KU-175-738

Top 25 locator map
(continues on inside
back cover)

◄

CityPack
Hong Kong

JOSEPH LEVY SHEENAN

If you have any comments
or suggestions for this guide
you can contact the editor at
Citypack@theAA.com

AA Publishing
Find out more about AA Publishing and the wide
range of services the AA provides by visiting our
website at *www.theAA.com/bookshop*

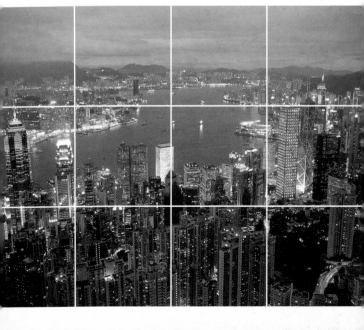

About This Book

KEY TO SYMBOLS

➕ Map reference to the accompanying fold-out map and Top 25 locator map

✉ Address

☎ Telephone number

🕐 Opening/closing times

🍴 Restaurant or café on premises or nearby

🚉 Nearest railroad station

Ⓜ Nearest subway (tube) station

🚌 Nearest bus route

⛴ Nearest riverboat or ferry stop

♿ Facilities for visitors with disabilities

✋ Admission charges: Expensive (over HK$15), Moderate (HK$8–HK$15) and Inexpensive (under HK$8)

↔ Other nearby places of interest

❓ Other practical information

➤ Indicates the page where you will find a fuller description

ℹ Tourist information

ORGANIZATION

This guide is divided into six chapters:
- Planning Ahead, Getting There
- Living Hong Kong—Hong Kong Now, Hong Kong Then, Time to Shop, Out and About, Walks, Hong Kong by Night
- Hong Kong's Top 25 Sights
- Hong Kong's Best—best of the rest
- Where To—detailed listings of restaurants, hotels, shops and nightlife
- Travel Facts—practical information

In addition, easy-to-read side panels provide extra facts and snippets, highlights of places to visit and invaluable practical advice.

The colors of the tabs on the page corners match the colors of the triangles aligned with the chapter names on the contents page opposite.

MAPS

The fold-out map in the wallet at the back of this book is a comprehensive street plan of Hong Kong. The first (or only) grid reference given for each attraction refers to this map. **The Top 25 locator map** found on the inside front and back covers of the book itself is for quick reference. It shows the Top 25 Sights, described on pages 26–50, which are clearly plotted by number (**1**–**25**, not page number) across the city. The second map reference given for the Top 25 Sights refers to this map.

Contents

PLANNING AHEAD, GETTING THERE $4 - 7$

LIVING HONG KONG $8 - 24$

HONG KONG'S TOP 25 SIGHTS $25 - 50$

1 Po Lin Buddha *26*
2 Mai Po Marshes *27*
3 Sam Tung Uk Museum *28*
4 University Museum *29*
5 Che Kei Shan (Victoria Peak) *30*
6 Tai Ping Shan Street *31*
7 Bonham Strand *32*
8 Man Mo Temple *33*
9 Central Market *34*
10 Botanical & Zoological Gardens *35*
11 Exchange Square *36*
12 Lei Cheng Uk Museum *37*
13 Statue Square *38*
14 Hong Kong Park *39*
15 Star Ferry *40*
16 Museum of History *41*
17 Ocean Park *42*
18 Temple Street *43*
19 Space Museum *44*
20 Museum of Art *45*
21 A Symphony of Lights *46*
22 Ten Thousand Buddhas Temple *47*
23 Wong Tai Sin Temple *48*
24 Kowloon Walled City Park *49*
25 Stanley *50*

HONG KONG'S BEST $51 - 62$

WHERE TO $63 - 88$

TRAVEL FACTS $89 - 93$

INDEX $94 - 95$

CREDITS AND ACKNOWLEDGMENTS 96

Planning Ahead

WHEN TO GO

The ideal time to visit is between October and mid-December, when the days are warm and fresh and the nights are cool and comfortable. Try to avoid June–September, when the weather is extremely hot and humid. The hotels are at their most expensive from late autumn until after the Chinese New Year in early February.

TIME

Hong Kong is 8 hours ahead of the UK, 13 hours ahead of New York and 16 hours ahead of Los Angeles.

AVERAGE DAILY MAXIMUM TEMPERATURES

JAN	FEB	MAR	APR	MAY	JUN	JUL	AUG	SEP	OCT	NOV	DEC
64°F	63°F	66°F	75°F	82°F	84°F	88°F	88°F	84°F	81°F	73°F	68°F
18°C	17°C	19°C	24°C	28°C	29°C	31°C	31°C	29°C	27°C	23°C	20°C

Spring (March through May) is usually warm, although rain is common.
Summer (June through September) is very hot and humid, with nearly 16 ins (400mm) of rain on average each month. The clammy heat sometimes gives way to violent typhoons.
Fall (October through to mid-December) is usually warm.
Winter (Mid-December through February) is comfortable, with occasional cold spells.
Typhoons hit Hong Kong between July and September. Hotels post the appropriate storm signal: Storm Signal 1=Typhoon within 500 miles (800km) of Hong Kong; Storm Signal 3=Typhoon on its way, be prepared; Storm Signal 8=Stay in your hotel, dangerous winds with gusts.

WHAT'S ON

January/February *Chinese (Lunar) New Year*: This family event looms large in Hong Kong life. The week before the New Year is busy; the harbor fireworks display is magnificent, but the crowds are enormous.
Mid-January/mid-March *Arts Festival*: International orchestral, dance and theater events over four weeks.
Late March/April *International Film Festival*: For two weeks; various venues.
April *Ching Ming*: Tomb-sweeping day.

Tin Hau Festival: Tin Hau temples (➤ 55) remember a 12th-century legend about a girl who saves her brother from drowning. Fishing junks and temples are decorated and Chinese street operas held near the temples.
Birthday of Lord Buddha (late April): At temples Buddha's statue is ceremonially bathed and scented symbolically washing away sins and material encumbrances.
June *Dragon Boat Festival*: Noisy, colorful dragon-boat races are enthusiastically

held to commemorate the political protests of a 4th-century poet and patriot, Chu Yuan.
August/September *Hungry Ghosts Festival*: Offerings of food are set out to placate roaming spirits (➤ 37).
September/October *Mid-Autumn Festival*: Families head out with lanterns and eat mooncakes to commemorate a 14th-century uprising against the Mongols.
October/November *Festival of Asian Arts*: Asian music, dance and theater in even-numbered years.

HONG KONG ONLINE

www.discoverhongkong.com
The official website of the Hong Kong Tourist Board. Lots of general information about Hong Kong, suggestions for day trips, family days out, history, information on transport etc.

www.bcmagazine.net
The website of the free magazine of the same name. Lots of information on what's on, restaurant reviews, shopping tips, all aimed at a younger audience.

www.gayhk.com
Information about Hong Kong's gay scene, attitudes in the territory, good places to visit, reviews of clubs, bars and more.

www.scmp.com.hk
This is the site of the *South China Morning Post*, the territory's independent newspaper. News items, cultural information, current affairs. Gives an insight into what concerns Hong Kongers.

www.info.gov.hk
The Hong Kong government's Information Services Department website. Another angle on all the sights—good on parks and museums.

www.skybird.com.hk
Information and prices for tours of this recognized company in the city.

www.grayline.com.hk
A well-established tour company gives details of tours of the island and trips into China and Taiwan.

www.hongkongairport.com
The site of Hong Kong International Airport. Lots of useful information before you actually arrive.

www.hkclubbing.com
This site keeps track of the new and not so new clubs in the city. Reviews from locals, details of opening hours and prices, lots of opinion.

GOOD TRAVEL SITES

www.fodors.com
A complete travel-planning site. You can research prices and weather; book air tickets, cars and rooms; ask questions (and get answers) from fellow travelers; and find links to other sites.

www.mtr.com.hk
Information on the metro system in Hong Kong. Details of Octopus cards, airport express, tourist passes, many other useful details.

CYBERCAFÉS

Coffee 'n Books
🞦 F6 ✉ 67 Mody Road, Shop 104, Peninsula Centre, Tsim Sha Tsui
☎ 2723 0488 🕐 Mon–Sat 8am–midnight, Sun 10am–midnight
💷 HK$10 for 30 minutes

Pacific Coffee Company
🞦 E8 ✉ Food Hall, LG/F Seibu Department Store, Pacific Place, 88 Queensway, Admiralty
☎ 2918 9778
🕐 7.30am–8pm
💷 Free with purchase of coffee

Getting There

ENTRY REQUIREMENTS

All visitors must hold a valid passport. The length of a visa-free visit depends on citizenship: six months for British citizens; one month for American, German and Greek citizens; three months for Commonwealth and most European citizens. All other citizens should consult the Chinese Embassy in their country.

MONEY

The unit of currency is the Hong Kong dollar (= 100 cents). Notes comes in denominations of 10, 20, 50, 100, 500 and 1,000; coins are 10, 20 and 50 cents.

$50

$100

$500

$1000

ARRIVING

All flights land at Hong Kong International Airport at Chek Lap Kok 24 miles (39km) west of Hong Kong city. The eight floors of the airport include three banks, a moneychanger, several ATMs, a tourist information office and acres of restaurants and bars.

ARRIVING AT CHEK LAP KOK AIRPORT

For airport information ☎ 2181 0000; www.hkairport.com.

The Airport Express (☎ 2881 8888, www.mtr.com.hk) is the most efficient and pleasant way of getting to town from the airport. Trains depart for the city at ten-minute intervals from 5.50am to 12.50am; journey time to Central is 23 minutes, to Kowloon 18 minutes; cost HK$100 one way to/from Central, HK$90 to/from Kowloon. A same-day return is the same as a single fare.

There are also bus services into Hong Kong Island, Kowloon, the New Territories and Lantau which are much cheaper. Information on times and prices can be obtained from the tourist office in the airport. The Citybus A11 travels into Hong Kong Island for HK$40, while the A21 serves Kowloon for HK$33.

A taxi to Hong Kong Island is the expensive option and will cost around HK$335. This includes the toll fare for the Lantau Link, the bridge which joins Lantau Island to Hong Kong Island. The journey to Kowloon costs around HK$270.

ARRIVING BY BUS OR TRAIN

Visas are required to cross the border into the mainland, available from the Visa Office of the People's Republic of China, 7/F Lower Block, China Resources Center, 26 Harbour Road, Wanchai, ☎ 3413 2300, 9am–noon, 2–5pm.

Bus companies running services into China include: CTS Express Coaches, 138 Hennessy Road, Wanchai, ☎ 2764 9803, www.ctsbus.hkcts.com. Eternal East Cross Border Coach, Shop G11, G/F Hankow Centre, ☎ 2723 2923.

High-speed trains travel from Hung Hom station to Guangzhou several times a day. There are also rail links to Shanghai and Beijing. Tickets can be booked up to 60 days in advance from the station in Hung Hom or by phone, ☎ 2947 7888.

GETTING AROUND

Traveling by bus is not recommended (except for trips to the south side of Hong Kong Island); the MTR train network is faster and easier to use. The MTR is the quickest way to hop between shopping areas, between Hong Kong Island and TST; for access to the New Territories use the interchange station at Kowloon Tong and change to the KCR (Kowloon Canton Railway), which travels north to the border at Lo Wu.

Stations have clear instructions in both English and Chinese for operating ticket machines. Machines issue thin plastic cards that are also available from information/ticket counters. Fares are between HK$4 and HK$12.50. Tickets have a magnetic strip and the fare is deducted automatically as you pass through the ticket barrier. For inquiries ☎ 2881 8888.

MTR maps are available at the airport and most hotel lobbies. MTR stations dispense a free guide to the system in English and Chinese. Tourist Board offices have a free map showing bus fares and routes.

Taxis are good value and can be picked up at ranks throughout the city, although many drivers do not speak English. Once inside you must use the seat belt.

For more information on getting around, including discounts and trams ► 91–92.

► 91–92.

INSURANCE

It is vital to have cover for medical expenses and accidents, as well as theft, baggage loss and trip cancellation.
Check your insurance coverage and buy a supplementary policy as needed.

VISITORS WITH DISABILITIES

Generally speaking wheelchair users will find that the newer buildings have good access while older buildings and most streets, MTR stations, footbridges, of which there are hundreds, and shopping centers are difficult to negotiate. Taxis, ferries and some buses are wheelchair friendly. Joint Council for the Physically and Mentally Disabled Rm. 1204, 31 Hennessy Rd, Wanchai, ☎ 2864 2931, www.hkcss.org.hk

Living
Hong Kong

Hong Kong Now *10–15*

Hong Kong Then *16–17*

Time to Shop *18–19*

Out and About *20–21*

Walks *22–23*

Hong Kong by Night *24*

Hong Kong Now

Above: *View across Repulse Bay*

First-time visitors come to Hong Kong with vague impressions of kung-fu movies, red-sailed junks gliding past high-rise office blocks in Victoria Harbour, crowded streets and soaring skyscrapers, but the reality of the city will surpass your expectations. Beautiful, crass, frenetic, raucous, grimy and serenely peaceful by turns, the tiny city and its satellite islands, suburbs and countryside are a shock to the system of the most hardened world traveler. Hong Kong has all the attributes of a whole country—character, culture, sights, bars, shopping—but condensed, packed into one tiny pocket handkerchief of an island.

NEIGHBORHOODS

- **Central**: The administrative center of the city. Sightseeing, theaters, entertainment.
  Lan Kwai Fong and Soho: The fun heart of the city with lots of bars, clubs and cafés.
  Causeway Bay: The most popular shopping district for locals.
  Aberdeen: The home of Ocean Park and floating restaurants.
  Tsim Sha Tsui (TST): The tourist heartland, pubs and clubs, theaters and swanky hotels.
  New Territories: The green lung of the city with interesting sights and museums, and the border with mainland China.

VITAL STATISTICS

● Hong Kong has a population of 7 million.
● 80 percent of Hong Kong's territory is rural or country park.
● Hong Kong has the world's largest indoor Chinese restaurant, the Ocean City Restaurant, which can serve more than 6,000 guests.
● Hong Kong has the highest per capita ownership of Rolls Royce cars in the world.

The dynamo that charges the city with life is its people. Hong Kongers are an amazing group of people, resilient, hard working, hard nosed; they have had to be. In the last eight years this little economic honey pot has been through the wringer. The regime change that took place in 1997 when British colonials gave way to emerging Chinese capitalists was followed by three major epidemics, an economic recession that hit Asia hard, and serious deflation which wiped millions of dollars off the property market and people's savings—the two things that ordinary people relied on for their future—and all this in a country that, even when it was pouring cash into the British economy, never had a minimum wage, democracy or a social security system. The city's industrial areas have pretty much shipped out to Shenzen and Shanghai and thousands of people who were able to claim passports from another country—Britain, Canada, Australia, the US—have left to be replaced by mainland Chinese. Locals quickly came to realize that the newcomers came from a very different culture from their own. Only time will tell how the situation will continue to develop.

Above: *Peak Tower*
Above right: *The "Forever Blooming" Bauhinia sculpture*

Of the nearly 7 million citizens of the Special Administrative Region (SAR), the overwhelming majority (94 percent) is Chinese, although hanging out in Lan Kwai Fong in the evenings you'd find this difficult to believe. Hong Kong Chinese are a fascinating mix of 21st-century hi-tech and ancient beliefs. A stunning new office block's workers will decorate their workspace with feng shui objects, put mirrors and plants in to catch the good chi as it passes through, and even the architects will have

SARS

• Severe Acute Respiratory Syndrome found its way into Hong Kong through China and did damage to the city's lifestyle and economy far in excess of the real threat to human life which it represented. The city came to a virtual standstill with schools closed, the streets empty and those forced to go out donning face masks. The government responded instantly, searching for the origin of the outbreak, disinfecting old housing and testing the temperatures of office workers and students on a daily basis. Even so many left and tourism and business trips came to a complete stop and it was months before normal life resumed. Some even believed there was a mainland plot to associate the epidemic with Hong Kong and so drive business to Shanghai, Hong Kong's new economic rival. It is worth noting that for the world panic attack that took place over SARS, of the 1,755 people who caught the virus in Hong Kong, 1,455 recovered.

Above: *Old neighborhood alongside Central Plaza*

consulted a master to establish the most propitious shape, layout and position for the building. Along any street in town, especially during some of the festivals, little shrines dedicated to ancestors will be propped up on the street, perhaps outside a fast-food franchise joint. Walking in some of the housing complexes you may encounter an old lady beating with her shoe a piece of paper on which are written the names of her gossiping neighbors. This is the magic ritual of *da siu yan* (beating small people) with which she hopes to crush their malicious influence. All over the island you can see shops

GWEILOS

• The literal translation for *gweilo* is "ghost man" (*gweipor* means "ghost woman"), originally coined as a derogatory label for the pale-faced colonial masters. You can tell by the tone of voice if it is still meant in a derogatory manner, but usually nowadays it is used as a general reference for Westerners whose presence in areas such as Wan Chai, especially at night, seems disproportionate given that they constitute less than 2 percent of the population.

FILTH

• If *gweilo* has become an acceptable, even semi-affectionate, term for white office workers, FILTH is a slightly edgier term. It is an English acronym to describe the young, or not so young, Europeans who pose in their business suits after work in the bars of Lan Kwai Fong and who are resented a little for their excellent terms of employment, easy promotions and frequent paid leave. It stands for Failed In London, Try Hong Kong.

13

Above: *Visitors practising tai chi in the park*

selling funeral goods: paper and cardboard replicas of everyday items that are burned and sent up to the ancestors for their use in heaven. Once upon a time the replicas were furniture, money, clothes, but now the shops sell replica DVD players, mobile phones and Filipina maids.

Hong Kong's Chinese are not by any means a homogeneous group. Although they are chiefly of Cantonese descent and speak the same dialect, there are still enormous differences of class, wealth and culture. On the island live sophisticated, English-educated, wealthy folk who look to the West for their culture, while on the outlying islands and in the New Territories are people whose lives differ very little from those of

THE 14K AND THE BAMBOO UNION

• The names of the Triad Secret Societies may sound intriguing, but the reality of life in these secret societies is sordid. Promised easy money and social acceptance, disaffected youths of both sexes are lured into these groups, which control organized crime in Hong Kong. Unless they leave very soon, they are drawn into an organization with a lifetime membership. While triads are thriving in Hong Kong it is unlikely tourists or even expats will encounter them.

Above: *Taking part in a Hong Kong festival*

rural China. About 55,000 mainland Chinese arrive and settle each year in search of economic opportunities and many are from a very different culture to the dominant one they encounter here. About 60,000 of Hong Kong's citizens are non-Chinese, largely ethnically Indian or from other countries in the region. When Hong Kong became the SAR it was decided that passports for the new region would only be issued to Chinese permanent residents so that all other races, regardless of the length of time their families had been settled in the region, became stateless.

After its shaky early years Hong Kong is back on track. With its industrial heartland gone it has had to focus on hi-tech industries and that seems to be making the island a cleaner and greener place with less air pollution and spotless beaches. New projects have given foreign investors the confidence to bring their money back and there are plans to extend the KCR, the rail link into the New Territories, into Shenzen and connect the island to China and beyond. The *gweilos* (Westerners), remain in residence, having a good time in the city before going back home to settle down.

LIVE TO WORK

• The work ethic is not an ideal in Hong Kong, it is simply a necessity of life. There are virtually no natural resources, only some 390sq miles (1,000sq km) of land, and no unemployment pay or minimum wages.

15

Hong Kong Then

Above from left: A detail from the Lei Cheng Uk tomb; British royal insignia on post box; hillside grave on Lamma Island; Murray House

4000BC Early settlement left some pottery, stone tools and iron implements— then for many centuries the islands had more pirates than farmers.

c200BC The Chinese Empire is unified and for the next millennium-and-a-half Hong Kong Island is ruled by a governor based in Canton.

1685 British and French merchants begin to deal in tea and silk. The British later start to import opium as a way of extending their power and profits.

1841 Chinese attempts to block the import of opium end in defeat; the treaty concluding the first Opium War cedes Hong Kong Island to the British "in perpetuity." Within two decades, another treaty concedes the Kowloon Peninsula. In 1889 a further treaty leases substantial land north of Kowloon—the New Territories—to Britain for 99 years.

1941–45 Japanese occupation (▶ side panel).

1949 The Communist victory in China leads to refugee influxes.

1950–53 When the US imposes sanctions against China during the Korean War the colony develops a manufacturing base of its own.

WORLD WAR II

In 1937, hundreds of thousands of Chinese, displaced by the Japanese invasion of China, sought refuge in Hong Kong. On 8 December 1941, Japanese aircraft bombed Kowloon, and by Christmas Day the British had surrendered. More than 2,000 people died and 10,000 soldiers were taken prisoner. British civilians were incarcerated in Stanley Prison. With the surrender of the Japanese in August 1945, Hong Kong again became a British colony.

1967 The political passions rocking China spill over into Hong Kong, with riots and strikes. The colony seems on the brink of a premature closure of its lease, but normality soon returns.

1975 100,000 Vietnamese refugees arrive.

1982 British Prime Minister Margaret Thatcher goes to Beijing to discuss the colony's future.

1984 The Sino-British Joint Declaration confirms the return of the colony to China. In 1988 Beijing publishes its Basic Law for Hong Kong citizens, guaranteeing their rights.

1989 The Tiananmen Square massacre confirms Hong Kong's worst fears about the future under China's sovereignty. Over one million people protest on the streets of Hong Kong.

1997 Hong Kong becomes a Special Administrative Region of China. English remains an official language. People from other parts of China require special approval for entry.

1998 Turmoil in Asian stock markets delivers a blow to Hong Kong.

2003 SARS epidemic disrupts life on the island.

THE HANDOVER

At midnight on 30 June 1997, Britain's last vestige of empire was handed back to the Chinese. Trepidation surrounded the occasion, but in the event it was a muted affair in one of the worst rainstorms in memory. Few people were on the streets. Chris Patten, Hong Kong's last governor, and Prince Charles quietly and tearfully slipped away on the royal yacht *Britannia* and the Red Army silently drove across the border. The expatriate workers who had not chosen to leave marked the occasion in Lan Kwai Fong bars, and everyone woke up the next day a little nervously, wondering how their lives would be changed, and a little shocked that nothing seemed different.

Time to Shop

Below: *Sale time in the city.*
Below right: *Ladies' Market.
Mong Kok*

A huge part of the fun of a trip to Hong Kong is shopping. Among locals it is a way of life rather than a trip to get necessities. One reason to shop in Hong Kong is that many items such as

cameras, electronics, clothes, shoes and glasses can be cheaper here than in Europe. American visitors might pick up a few bargains too, but if you want to buy something be aware of the price at home. Be aware too, that on large new items you may be charged import duties on your return home and there is the inconvenience of getting things back undamaged. Also see the shopping section (► 75, 76) for advice on guarantees and possible rip-offs.

The most popular items with visitors are in the big Chinese emporiums and flea markets. Look out for hand-embroidered silk shawls and blouses, Chinese slippers, all kinds of silk cushion covers and bedspreads. There are lots of tailors in Hong Kong who can make suits or shirts within a few days at relatively inexpensive prices. For bargain hunters there are many factory shops and outlets where all kinds of seconds and end-of-run clothes are available at a fraction of the retail price. However, these places need some determined assessing and you should be

SAFE SHOPPING

The Hong Kong Tourist Board, no doubt fed up with tourist complaints about rip-offs, has produced an excellent booklet called *A Guide to Quality Shops and Restaurants* which lists all the places which have qualified under its scheme called QTS. It's a little hefty to stick in your handbag but it is very useful if you intend to do some serious shopping.

prepared for bad days when there is little worth buying. Another serious contender for your vacation funds is jewelry, either made with semiprecious stones or cloisonné, or the really

Below left: *Shopping in Pacific Place*

expensive stuff made with diamonds and precious stones. Gold jewelry is beautifully made, often using Chinese characters as a design feature. Hong Kong is a great place to buy jade and the tourist board organizes an hour-long seminar on how to look for the best jade.

Ceramics are also an excellent purchase with both Chinese and western dinner services, teapots in hand-made basket cozies and abstract pottery. Chinese cooking utensils are cheap to buy in the wetmarkets and are very useful and visually interesting. Also pretty and unusual are bamboo steaming baskets for vegetables and tiffin carriers—stacked metal containers for carrying your lunch to work. Inexpensive and difficult to get outside of Chinese communities are Chinese dried goods and herbal remedies such as ginseng, dried fish such as abalone and shark's fin and even birds' nest. Chinese tea is also a good buy. Kites and wooden toys are excellent too, and there are crafts from other parts of Asia that are also attractively priced.

BARGAINING

Bargaining is an essential part of the shopping skills of the Hong Konger. They are of little use in department stores or other fixed-price establishments but in the markets or smaller shops bargaining is essential. A good idea when bargaining is to know roughly how much the item costs in a fixed-price shop and aim to conclude a deal at a slightly lower price than that. Try a few practice bargains first to get the hang of it and be aware that, especially in highly touristy areas, the stallholder may assume you have no idea of the value of an item and ask for far too much on the off chance that you'll fall for it. Also be aware of the advice on rip-offs in the shopping section (► 75, 76), especially if the shopkeeper goes to the back to pack your item for you.

Out and About

HERITAGE TOUR

The Man Mo Temple in Tai Po (► 33), part of the HKTB's Heritage Tour, is an especially rich experience on a Saturday, when the surrounding street market is abuzz. The ancient gray stone temple, dedicated to the gods of war and literature, offers a calm respite from the market outside. In the market, look for the snakes in the snake soup shops, the partially dissected live fish in the fish stalls and old ladies carrying their wares suspended from a pole across their shoulders.

INFORMATION

MACAU
Distance 37 miles (60km)
Journey Time 1 hour by jetfoil
🚢 Jetfoil from the Shun Tak Centre ✚ D7
✉ 200 Connaught Road
💵 HK$130–161
ℹ In Macau: Largo do Senado, Edificio Ritz No. 9
☎ (853) 315 566. In Hong Kong: Shop 336, Shun Tak Centre, 200 Connaught Road, Central
☎ 2857 2287
📘 Take your passport; no visa required for North Americans or Europeans staying 20 days or less

ORGANIZED SIGHTSEEING

The **Hong Kong Tourist Board** (► 91) conducts tours to a number of destinations, as well as themed tours. **Splendid** organizes personalized tours of Hong Kong and South China, including an Aberdeen or harbor night cruise, horseracing

(June–September), Lantau Island and a Splendid Night of delight. They also do tours into China (☎ 2316 2151; www.splendidtours.com 💵 HK $280). **Water Tours Ltd**. conducts nearly 20 different harbor cruises, including a Sampan ride around Aberdeen (☎ 2926 3868; www.water tourshk.com). **Star Ferry** runs seven ferries a day (☎ 2366 7024), while **Grayline Tours** offers city tours, dinner cruises and day trips to China (☎ 2368 7111).

EXCURSIONS
MACAU

Cobbled streets, baroque architecture and the traditional cuisine and wines of Portugal's last colony are good reasons for taking the trip to Macau, which reverted to China in December 1999. Macau is compact and most of the main places of interest you can take in in a day. Highlights include the ruined façade of 17th-century St. Paul's Church, the Jesuit Monte Fortress and a number of old churches and temples. Hotels and good restaurants are easy to find, and prices are agreeably lower than those in Hong Kong.

NEW TERRITORIES

The New Territories are best explored via the Kowloon–Canton Railway (➤ 7). From Kowloon the line heads north, stopping at many interesting places. From either Tai Po Market station or Tai Wo station, take a taxi to the Hong Kong Railway

Museum and visit the Man Mo Temple, Tai Po, in the adjacent pedestrianized market street. At the next station, Fanling, take the right exit; the Taoist Ying Sin Kwun Temple across the road is worth a visit, as is the village just minutes from the next station, Sheung Shui. Take the overhead walkway to the right and head down to the bus station. With McDonald's on your right, walk along the main road until you see the old lanes on the left. Life here, only a few miles south of the border, is similar to the rest of China.

THE PEOPLE'S REPUBLIC OF CHINA

The Beijing government has designated Shenzen as a Special Economic Zone, and tourists and investors—anyone with money to spend—are welcomed with open arms. Here you'll find Splendid China, a theme park where the Great Wall, the Forbidden City and other monuments of Chinese architecture are reduced to one-fifteenth real size. The nearby China Folk Culture Village introduces the country's ethnic minorities. Guangzhou (Canton) is a major city and port on the Pearl River. It offers an astonishing food market, a 100BC royal tomb and several temples.

Below from left: *City skyline; Heritage Museum, Shatin*

INFORMATION

NEW TERRITORIES
Distance Tai Po 15.5 miles (25km); Sheung Shui 22 miles (35km)
Journey Time Tai Po 30 minutes; Sheung Shui 1 hour
🚇 MTR from any station to Kowloon Tong (➕ F2), then KCR train traveling north to Lo Wu. The last stop is Sheung Shui; this is as far as you can go without entering China.
Hong Kong Railway Museum
🕐 Wed–Mon 9–4

INFORMATION

THE PEOPLE'S REPUBLIC OF CHINA
Shenzen can be seen in a day, while Guangzhou (Canton) is best enjoyed with an overnight stay. You *must* have a visa, issued in Hong Kong. Grayline runs tours to both destinations (➤ 20).
Shenzen
Distance 25miles (40km)
Journey Time 40 minutes
🚉 KCR from Kowloon Tong to border at Lo Wu
Guangzhou (Canton)
Distance 75 miles (120km) **Journey Time** 3 hours 🚉 Express from Hong Kong

Walks

THE SIGHTS

- Bowen Road shrines
- Mid Levels
- Lover's Stone Garden
- Police Museum
- Covered market
- Meat and fish stalls along Wan Chai Road

INFORMATION

Distance 1.5 miles (3km)
Time 2 hours
Start point ★ Bowen Road
🚻 G10
🚌 15 from Central Bus Terminal or Peak Terminal; get off at the Adventist Hospital at the horseshoe bend where Bowen Road meets Stubbs Road
End point Johnston Road
🚻 F8
🚇 Wan Chai
🚋 Tram stop on Johnston Road

ALONG THE QUIET MID LEVELS OF THE PEAK, THEN INTO HECTIC WAN CHAI

Shady and quiet, Bowen Road runs along the Mid Levels on Hong Kong Island, a residential area halfway up Victoria Peak; note the small roadside shrines. Walk west for 15 minutes, then look for steps on the left up to an exposed rock shrine (Lover's Stone Garden) via a small complex of incense-burning pots. Continue along Bowen Road as far as Wan Chai Gap Road. Detour left, to Stubbs Road and the Police Museum. Or continue right, along the main walk, down steep Wan Chai Gap Road. At the bottom, turn right into Kennedy Road and then left into Queen's Road East. Turn right at the covered market—with plenty of bargains to be had—into bustling Wan Chai Road.

Turn left into Johnston Road; pause for traditional herbal tea at No. 137, next to the Simsons Commercial Building. For lunch, try Indian cuisine at the International Curry House in Tai Wong Street East, or at the Jo Jo Mess Club (► 68) with its good-value, reliable food, entered on Lee Tung Street, both left turns off Johnston Road.

One block to the south is Hennessy Road, where there are plenty of fast-food eateries.

THE HEART OF HONG KONG

Start this walk at Western Market, once the local "wet," or fresh food, market, opposite Macau Ferry Pier on Hong Kong Island; built in 1906 and renovated in 1991, it is now dedicated to arts and crafts. Head south, uphill, then turn right into Wing Lok Street, a traditional trading street with neon signs, aging buildings and a variety of flourishing trades. Turning back along Bonham Strand West, notice the flashy new ginseng wholesalers that still have huge traditional lanterns and painted signboards.

Inspect the food on sale in Sheung Wan Market; for an adventure, visit the top floor and sample some local dishes. Along Bonham Strand East and Queen's Road West there are many antiques shops and shops selling calligraphy materials, wedding clothes and also funeral paraphernalia. Queen's Road has the big stores.

At Peel Street, turn uphill and wander through the street market, which sells all manner of foreign things. Turn right into Hollywood Road, part of Sheung Wan, and admire the applied arts shops. The Man Mo Temple is in this road; turn right down Ladder Street, which leads to Upper Lascar Row and more antiques, curios and junk merchants. From here, go downhill to return to the walk's starting point, taking in on the way Possession Street, where the British flag was first raised.

THE SIGHTS

- Western Market
- Bonham Strand ginseng traders (► 32)
- Sheung Wan Market
- Bonham Strand East antique shops
- Man Mo Temple (► 33)
- Possession Street

INFORMATION

Distance 1.5 miles (3km)
Time 2 hours
Start/end point
★ Western Market
⊞ D7
🚇 Sheung Wan
🚊 Any tram from Central

Below: *Provisions and dried foods for sale in Sheung Wan*
Below left: *Gloucester Road, Wan Chai*

Hong Kong by Night

Above: *Floating restaurants in Aberdeen*
Above centre: *Man Mo Temple*
Above right: *Nathan Road by night*

HOSTESS CLUBS

Wandering into the bars in Lan Kwai Fong you will notice that lots of these bars are inhabited by pretty young girls who get a commission for each expensive drink they can persuade a customer to buy them. Their purpose in the bar is to keep customers there and spending money and as long as all parties know it, no one ends up disappointed. In TST and Wan Chai there are dedicated hostess bars where you are charged for talking to the girls in the form usually of a huge entrance fee or ludicrously expensive drinks.

WITH THE IN CROWD

The place to be in Hong Kong for a good time at night is Hong Kong Island and in particular Lan Kwai Fong where the FILTH (► 13) hangs out. It is an area of older buildings, once pretty sleazy but now clean, pedestrianized and full of expensive bars and clubs. Its bars are inhabited by young, bespoke men and women, fresh from a day's money-making in front of a monitor in an office and ready to party. Farther west is Soho with lots of classy restaurants and some bars.

RELAXING

To the east Wan Chai was traditionally the base for sleazy clubs during the days of the Vietnam war. It is slightly more respectable now, with hostess bars charging an arm and a leg for a beer, but also some good clubs and bars. Wan Chai is home to some nice relaxed pubs if all you're after is a quiet drink.

PARTY WITH THE LOCALS

Kowloon also offers places to drink especially in the touristy Tsim Sha Tsui (TST) where there are hostess bars and clubs around Knutsford Terrace as well as a couple of good places for a relatively inexpensive drink. The area is a little run down these days, but if you want to mingle with locals without a trip out to the New Territories this is the place to do it. Bars generally open around midday and close after 2am, while clubs open from around 6pm till around 1am on weekdays and as late as 4am at weekends. Most have a happy hour lasting for up to three hours in the early evening.

HONG KONG's
top 25 sights

The sights are shown on the maps on the inside front cover and inside back cover, numbered **1**–**25** from west to east across the city

1 Po Lin Buddha *26*

2 Mai Po Marshes *27*

3 Sam Tung Uk Museum *28*

4 University Museum *29*

5 Che Kei Shan (Victoria Peak) *30*

6 Tai Ping Shan Street *31*

7 Bonham Strand *32*

8 Man Mo Temple *33*

9 Central Market *34*

10 Botanical & Zoological Gardens *35*

11 Exchange Square *36*

12 Lei Cheng Uk Museum *37*

13 Statue Square *38*

14 Hong Kong Park *39*

15 Star Ferry *40*

16 Museum of History *41*

17 Ocean Park *42*

18 Temple Street *43*

19 Space Museum *44*

20 Museum of Art *45*

21 A Symphony of Lights *46*

22 Ten Thousand Buddhas Temple *47*

23 Wong Tai Sin Temple *48*

24 Kowloon Walled City Park *49*

25 Stanley *50*

Po Lin Buddha

HIGHLIGHTS

- Po Lin Buddha
- Tranquil monastery
- Views of the South China Sea and other islands
- A peaceful ferry ride
- Museum of Buddah's life on second level of podium

INFORMATION

- Off map to west; Locator map C4
- Lantau Island
- Temple and museum: daily 10.30–5. Monastery: daily 9–6
- Tung Chung and then buses heading for Po Lin
- Ferry from Queen's Pier Central (journey time approx 45 minutes)
- Free **?** HKTB guided walks: Lantau Island–Tung Chung Valley

Asia's largest seated outdoor Buddha, the 112-ft (34-m) tall, 250-ton bronze statue sits atop a mountain on Lantau Island. You can spy the Buddha sitting in his meditative pose as you descend into Chek Lap Kok airport.

Worth the trek Even after the airport was built, Lantau remained one of the largest green areas in Hong Kong. It is home to rare species such as the Hong Kong newt and the ayu, a stream-dwelling fish. The island's rocky coastline and jungle mountain scenery make it a bit of an outback. But this isolated outpost is home to almost 300 Buddist monasteries, most of them tiny temples tucked away in remote areas. The famous Po Lin Buddha is at Po Lin (Precious Lotus) Monastery, halfway up the mountainside on the Ngong Ping Plateau. Established by three monks in 1905 the monastery is now extensively restored. But the real attraction is the huge Buddha, which was completed in 1993 on the hilltop above the monastery. To get up close, you need to climb 268 steps. Up top, you get a splendid view of Lantau and the other little islands dotting the blue-jade South China Sea. There are also trails jutting away from the monastery if you want to go for a longer walk.

Go now On Buddist holidays up to 13,000 visitors a day make the trek to the Buddha. But at other times, the island feels quite remote, despite the airport (constructed in 1998), which brought a train connection to Kowloon and Hong Kong Island; before then, you could reach the island only by ferry. Now, with plans afoot for developing housing on the island and the opening of a Disney theme park proposed for 2006, there are fears for the ecology and the remoteness of the area.

Mai Po Marshes

On the edge of mainland China and framed by the hazy, fume-filled skyline of Shenzen, the internationally protected Mai Po Marsh is home to thousands of rare and endangered birds—get some binoculars to view.

Nature reserve The marsh, on the edge of Deep Bay, in the northwest of the New Territories covers about 3, 706 acres (1,500ha) of wetlands. At its heart is the 939-acre (380-ha) nature reserve where during the winter months as many as 300 different species of migratory birds have been recorded. Bird life is plentiful all year round with indigenous species, including several types of kingfisher, long-tailed shrike, Japanese white-eye, and plain and yellow-bellied prinias. Much of the area is salt marsh filled with mangrove swamp, in whose roots live tiny crabs and shrimp that provide the food for the teeming bird life. Also fairly common in the reserve are leopard cats and otters.

Threatened birds Some seriously endangered species can be seen here with a bit of luck, including some that are numbered in only hundreds worldwide such as the black-faced spoonbill, Dalmatian pelican or imperial eagle.

Take a tour The visitor center has information and maps of the area explaining the history and ecology of the place. Out in the reserve itself are hides where you can watch the animals feeding, and floating boardwalks to take you out into the mudflats and mangroves. A good way to visit the reserve is to go with a private tour group who will drive around the reserve itself to more remote spots, including disused fishing ponds and lagoons, going at times over the border to hides deep within the marsh.

HIGHLIGHTS

- Rare and endangered species of birds
- Glimpses of leopard cats
- Mangrove swamps
- Floating boardwalks
- Views over Shenzen

INFORMATION

- ✚ Off map to north; Locator map off A3
- ✉ Mai Po
- ☎ 2471 8272
- 🕐 Daily 9–6
- 🚇 Sheung Shui then a taxi
- 🚌 76K from Fanling KCR station
- ♿ None
- 💷 Moderate
- ❓ Reserve a visit in advance since numbers are limited. Refundable deposit required. Binoculars can be rented at the visitor center

Sam Tung Uk Museum

HIGHLIGHTS

- Ancestral hall with ornate decorations
- Landscaped gardens
- Orientation room
- Blackwood furniture
- Cooking equipment
- Gatehouse of walled village
- Fish ponds
- Threshing floor

INFORMATION

- Off map to north; Locator map A3
- 2 Kwu Uk Lane, Tsuen Wan, New Territories
- 2411 2001
- Mon, Wed–Sun 9–5
- Tsuen Wan (exit E)
- Few
- Free
- HKTB Heritage tour (➤ 20), plus private tours

The clean, simple lines of this ancient Hakka dwelling stand out against the forest of high-rise housing blocks. Though simple farming people, the Hakka would have had far more space than their ancestors today.

History Around a million people now live in Tsuen Wan, which was a sleepy little waterside village of a few thousand souls until as recently as 1977. Back in the 17th century the area was subject to constant pirate attacks so the inhabitants built walled villages as a defense. Within each village lived the members of a single clan; a Hakka clan called the Chans made their home in Sam Tung Uk. The Hakka, originally from the north of China, moved to southern China in the 12th and 13th centuries, when the Chinese empire stretched to this area because the Chinese emperor was being driven south by invading Monguls. In 1277, the emperor and his entourage arrived in Tsuen Wan. Feuds over land tenure led some Hakka clans to migrate farther, to Hong Kong, Taiwan and Singapore. The village was probably built in 1786.

Three-beam dwelling This translation of the village's name refers to its structure. Three connected halls form the core of village life, and the three rows of houses were supported by three central beams called *tung*. The main ancestral hall is at the front and its design is highly ornate; its original decorations have been restored to their original bright reds and greens. The other two halls, used for daily living, are more rustic. These halls now display farming equipment, period furniture and kitchen utensils. Outside are a fish pond, a threshing floor and the gatehouse that guarded the village. The MTR journey out here takes at least one hour.

University Museum

This interesting little collection of predominantly Chinese artifacts is worth the effort to see it. Situated on the University of Hong Kong campus, it is usually blessedly empty.

Nestorian bronze crosses The displays in this out-of-the-way museum, in the university's Fung Ping Shan Building at the end of Bonham Road, date from the 5th century BC onwards, but the highlight is a set of 467 Nestorian bronze crosses—the largest such collection in the world—which belonged to a Christian sect that originated in Syria and came to China during the Tang Dynasty (AD618–906). The crosses date back to the Yuan Dynasty (1280–1367) and were probably worn as part of a belt or as a pendant. They are made in various cross shapes, including swastikas and birds, as well as conventional crucifixes.

Ceramics and bronzes Notable among the other bronze items on display are mirrors from the Warring States period (475–221BC), and Shang and Zhou ritual vessels and weapons. The museum also houses an enormous collection of ceramics dating back as far as neolithic times. The painted neolithic pottery is very fine, and the Han Dynasty horse is full of life. Look for the three-colour glaze Tang pottery, the famous kiln wares of Song and the polychrome and monochrome ceramics from the Ming and Qing dynasties.

Beyond Hong Kong Artifacts from other Asian countries include some Indian Buddhist sculptures and items from Thailand, Vietnam and Korea. Scroll paintings, inlaid blackwood furniture and a huge bronze drum make up the rest of the collection.

HIGHLIGHTS

- Nestorian bronze crosses
- Bronze mirrors
- Neolithic black pottery cup
- Pottery horse, Western Han Dynasty
- Qing Dynasty woodcarving
- Bronze drum
- Sui Dynasty spittoons
- Indian Buddhist sculptures
- Modern Chinese pottery from Jinghdezhen and Shiwan

INFORMATION

- B8; Locator map E4
- 94 Bonham Road, Hong Kong Island
- 2241 5500
- Mon–Sat 9.30–6, Sun 1.30–5.30. Closed public holidays and 16 March
- Sheung Wan
- 3B from Jardine House on Connaught Road or 23, 40, 40M from Pacific Place, Admiralty
- None
- Free

Che Kei Shan (Victoria Peak)

Visiting the Peak is one of the first things to do when you get to Hong Kong. At 1,811ft (552m) the hilltop views are spectacular and the area offers some peaceful, shady walks.

Head for heights Some people like to make the pilgrimage up the Peak twice—once during the day and again at night, when the full majesty of the city below is spelled out in lights. The Peak is a relatively unspoiled oasis in a concrete jungle, home of the rich and famous and a good place for a quiet walk or even a strenuous jog.

Top stop The Peak Galleria, is a veritable tourist trap. The Odditorium (400 displays of strange-but-true facts and artifacts), simulated rides, a wax museum and restaurants in the nearby Peak Tower offer further distractions. The trip up in the Peak Tram, constructed 1888, is good fun as long as you don't have to line up for it for hours—avoid weekends and the first day after a misty spell (and don't forget your camera). Feeding dollars into one of the telescopes is also worth the money on a clear day. From the tram stop you can also walk along Mount Austin Road to Victoria Park Gardens and the ruins of the Governor's Lodge, destroyed by the Japanese in World War II.

HIGHLIGHTS

- Views over Hong Kong
- Tram ride to the top
- Old Governor's Lodge, with toposcope in its gardens
- Souvenirs in Peak Galleria
- Outdoor tables in Peak Café
- Green-arrowed walk up Mount Austin Road

INFORMATION

- C9–D9; Locator map F4
- Peak Tower, Peak Road
- Peak Tram: runs 7am–midnight Odditorium: 9am–10pm
- Peak Galleria (snacks) and Peak Café
- Trams run every 10–15 minutes from terminals at Garden Road and Cotton Tree Drive. Central Bus 15C from Central Bus Terminal to Victoria Gap. 125 from Admiralty to lower tram terminus
- Good
- Tram fare: moderate Peak Tower: free Odditorium: moderate
- Botanical & Zoological Gardens (➤ 35), Hong Kong Park (➤ 39)

Souvenir shopping in the Peak Galleria

Tai Ping Shan Street

In many ways this street symbolizes the life of Hong Kong's ordinary citizens. At the eastern end are crowded apartment blocks; at the western end are peculiar little temples where you can still find the mystery of old Hong Kong.

Backstreet buildings South of Hollywood Road and its touristy antique and curio shops lies Tai Ping Shan Street, a quiet backwater of crumbling 1950s apartments, car-repair workshops and narrow, stepped alleys that lead north through street markets. At the western end, what seems to be a dead end becomes another narrow, stepped alley with tiny temples on either side.

Temple life Inside the temples, the atmosphere may seem, to an outsider, less than pious, with people shaking their fortunes out of bamboo pots to be read by interpreters, visitors bringing offerings of thanks and others just passing the time of day. However, nothing here is in English—these are serious places where a woman may come to ask for children or seek promotion at work. Like most temples in Hong Kong, these like to hedge their bets by paying homage to the Buddhist pantheon as well as to Taoist gods. Chinese religion is essentially pragmatic; if the gods turn up the goods then they must be paid. Around the temple stalls sell things the gods appreciate, such as joss sticks, incense candles, paper figures and fake paper or "hell" money to be burnt and sent up in smoke for the dead to spend in the next world.

HIGHLIGHTS

- Street temples with gold-painted doorway carvings
- Shops and stalls around temples
- Church in shopping block

INFORMATION

- C8; Locator map E3
- Tai Ping Shan Street, Sheung Wan
- Daily 8–8
- Cooked food stalls in nearby Sheung Wan Market
- Sheung Wan
- Trams run to Western Market from Central, Wan Chai and Causeway Bay
- Access difficult because of steep steps
- Temples free, but donations appreciated
- Bonham Strand (► 32)

Carving over temple door

31

Bonham Strand

HIGHLIGHTS

- Ginseng wholesalers on Bonham Strand West
- Chinese medicine shops in Ko Shing Street
- Street barbers in Sutherland Street
- Nearby Possession Street, marking the place where Hong Kong was claimed by the British
- Nearby Queen's Road West selling bird's nests
- Sheung Wan Market

INFORMATION

- D7; Locator map E3
- Bonham Strand, Sheung Wan
- Shops close on public holidays, particularly Chinese New Year
- Food stalls in Sheung Wan Market and streets around Bonham Strand; fast food near MTR station
- Sheung Wan
- Trams stop at Western Market and go on through Central to Causeway Bay
- Good
- Free
- Tai Ping Shan Street (➤ 28), Man Mo Temple (➤ 30)

Ginseng shops, antique markets, tiny lanes with ancient shops and the road where the British first set foot. Despite the renovations this area still recalls the old Hong Kong. The snake soup shops may be a thing of the past but many of the old ways still hang on.

Snake soup for sale The Bonham Strand area was once very much the old Hong Kong with tiny stepped streets filled with odd shops, some selling soups made from strange creatures such as snakes. Much of this is gone now but Bonham Strand West is still a fascinating place to visit for its ginseng shops. Nearby Hollywood Road is a series of trendy carpet and antique shops at its eastern end but farther west there are still coffin makers and paper goods shops selling everything the recently deceased need for the afterlife.

Bonham Strand West To reach the western half of Bonham Strand you need to walk down Wing Lok Street. This area is a great place to wander. Ginseng wholesalers share the road here with some prosperous-looking banks. Most of the quaint old wooden interiors of the former have now given way to glass and chrome, but the jars of unidentifiable items are still there. Ginseng means "man" in Chinese, so-called as the forked root resembles a person. Esteemed for its power as a universal panacea to heal and promote good health it is an expensive commodity and much wheeler-dealing goes on over its price. Different types of ginseng bring different prices, the American variety being the cheapest while ginseng from Korea and China is considered more efficacious and is therefore more expensive. Turn to the left off Bonham Strand West and you will find Queen's Road West with shops selling bird's nests—for the soup.

Man Mo Temple

The most remarkable aspects of this tiny, crumbling temple are the vast, and increasingly worn apartment blocks. Inside incense coils hung from the ceiling evoke a spiritual mood.

Taoism and Buddhism The temple represents an eclectic mix of the two religions, of which both have many adherents in Hong Kong. Like the Man Mo Temple in Tai Po (▶ 20), although substantially larger, this place is dedicated to two Taoist deities who represent the pen and the sword. These are Man, or Man Cheong, the god of literature; and Mo, or Kuan Ti, the god of war. The statues of Man and Mo are dressed lavishly in beautifully embroidered outfits. Beside the two main statues in the temple are representations of Pao Kung, the god of justice, and Shing Wong, the god who protects this region of the city. By the door are the figures of some lesser deities. A drum and a gong are sounded whenever an offering is made to the gods. The atmosphere seems almost casual—cats wander around, fortune-tellers peer into the future using bamboo sticks, and visitors place offerings of fruit or incense sticks in the offering boxes next to the statues inside the temple.

Nearby sights Next door, to the right, is the Litt Shing Kung, or All Saints Temple. Here too, you you can see people consulting the resident soothsayers, who interpret the *chim* (numbered bamboo sticks) tipped out of bamboo pots. The room to the left of the temple was once used as a schoolroom where free education was offered to the children of poor Chinese families. In the courtyard of the temple stand gilded plaques, carried in processions, while inside are the two 1862 sedan chairs used to convey the figures of the two gods.

HIGHLIGHTS

- Statues of Man Cheong and Kuan Ti
- Sedan chairs once used to carry statues
- Embroideries surrounding statues
- Drum and bell on right of entrance door
- Soot-blackened deities on left of entrance door
- Gold and brass standards carried during parades
- Resident fortune-tellers

INFORMATION

- D8; Locator map E3
- Junction of Hollywood Road and Ladder Street
- Daily 8–6
- Sheung Wan
- Access difficult
- Free
- Tai Ping Shan Street (▶ 28), Bonham Strand (▶ 32)

Central Market

HIGHLIGHTS

- Old-fashioned delivery bicycles
- Exotic green vegetables
- Strong-smelling durians
- Dried fish products
- Hawker stalls on top floor
- Beancurd product stalls

INFORMATION

✚ D8; Locator map E3
✉ Junction of Queen Victoria Street and Des Voeux Road
🕐 Daily 7–10, 5–8
🚇 Central
🚋 Trams from Sheung Wan, Wan Chai and Causeway Bay
⛴ Ferry from Tsim Sha Tsui
♿ None
🎟 Free
🔁 Exchange Square (➤ 36), Statue Square (➤ 38)

To appreciate fully just how different life is in Hong Kong, visit the places where people do their food shopping. Central Market sells some outrageous items, and the smell alone is exotic.

Layout This is one of Hong Kong's biggest fresh food, or "wet," markets and you should visit early, as most business is completed by mid-morning. The market is a large building on four floors on the junction beftween Queen Victoria Street and Des Voeux Road. The layout is very organized, with chicken and fish on one floor, red meats on another, and fruit and vegetables on yet another. There are about 300 stallholders in all, and the stock ranges from the prosaic to the peculiar—items such as salamanders and sea cucumbers.

What to look for Turtles are slaughtered to order—an especially gruesome sight—and other gory executions can be observed on the fish stalls. Scrotums are a delicacy sold in the meat hall, alongside tongues, intestines, ears and chicken feet (said to be especially good if cooked in mustard). Look for lotus root on the lower floors, a common vegetable that looks like Swiss cheese. In fall and winter the peculiar smell that rises above the other odours is not caused by a gas leak, but comes from the huge, spiky durian fruits stacked up on the fruit stalls—they have a custard-like texture and a flavor that is totally indescribable and most definitely an acquired taste. Not for the faint-hearted.

Botanical & Zoological Gardens

In the middle of this urban sprawl these gardens form a quiet little haven of peace. In fall, the scents of dazzling flowers fill the air and the wings of myriad butterflies shimmer in the light with a dazzling hue.

Oasis of calm This century-old complex, which once looked out over Victoria Harbour, is enclosed today by the city's towers (and bisected by a road; use the underpass to get from one part to the other). There are hundreds of species of birds, including many rare ones that breed happily in captivity. In the greenhouse are air plants, bromeliads and insectivorous plants such as pitcher plants, Venus fly-traps and rare butterworts. Early in the morning the gardens are full of people performing the slow exercise program know as *t'ai chi ch'uan*, which is designed to get the life forces flowing properly around the body. The zoo, though small, is surprisingly comprehensive and is also one of the world's leading centers for breeding endangered species.

Government House Opposite the gardens is Government House, where Hong Kong's British governors used to live. The house was built in 1855 and was added to through the years, perhaps one of the most attractive additions being the Japanese tower and roof corners that were put up during the Occupation. Government House is closed to the public, but you can peer through the gates or, if you are lucky, visit its gardens when they open for two days in March, when the azaleas are in bloom.

HIGHLIGHTS

- Bromeliads, air plants and carnivorous plants
- Amazing variety of butterflies, especially in fall
- Black jaguar
- Orangutan families
- Tree kangaroos from central New Guinea
- Flamingos
- Local people practising *t'ai chi chu'an*

INFORMATION

- D8; Locator map F3
- Several entrances; from Central the most accessible gate is on Upper Albert Road
- Botanic Gardens 2530 0154. Government House 2530 2003
- Daily 6am–10pm. Zoo and avaries: 6am–7pm. Greenhouses: 9–4.30
- Central
- 3, 12 from Connaught Road
- Snack kiosk
- Good ● Free

Many birds breed in the gardens

Exchange Square

HIGHLIGHTS

- Life-size bronze water buffalo statues
- Oversized statue of *t'ai chi ch'uan* practitioner
- Waterfront
- Henry Moore statue *Oval with Points*
- No. 1 Exchange Square

INFORMATION

- D8; Locator map E3
- Exchange Square, Central
- Central
- Café in the Forum; also fast food available on lower floors
- Good

The best times to visit this square and the surrounding areas are when they are busy—either at lunchtime when the people who work nearby are out getting their lunch, or on Sunday when the Filipina maids on their day off are picnicking with their friends.

The scene Exchange Square, designed by Hong Kong's P&T Architects in 1985, consists of several ultramodern tower blocks, including the Hong Kong Stock Exchange, linked to a series of overhead walkways to Shung Wan in the west. The square contains some of Central's more elegantly designed structures. The towers provide shade, the waterfalls the cooling sound of water, the statuary a sense of dignity and place. It can be a chilly spot, with brisk winds blowing in straight from the sea and channelled through the gaps between the buildings. The grand buildings are huge monoliths of smooth pink granite, quarried from one of Hong Kong's many hills.

Number 1 Take a look inside No. 1 Exchange Square. On the first floor you will find an exhibition gallery; the trip up the escalator takes you past another two stunning waterfalls. The overall effect of the square is very bleak. The scene is, however, considerably more cheerful on Sundays when the place is full of high-pitched noise and laughter and the picnickers fill every available spot.

Exchange Square

Lei Cheng Uk Museum

Though built over an ancient Han-dynasty tomb, this little museum is now surrounded by high-rise apartments occupied by thousands of Hong Kong people. This continuity between the living and the dead, spanning 2,000 years, is very moving.

Unique find The Lei Cheng Uk Museum is very modest in its appearance and layout, but it contains Hong Kong's oldest man-made structure. The tomb, built between AD25 and 220, consists of a central domed chamber with four barrel-roofed side chambers leading from it. The entranceway was destroyed before the tomb was noticed—accidentally, in 1955, when the housing development around it was being built.

Tomb objects No human remains were found, but inscriptions on the bricks wish goodwill and peace to the region and mark the name Master Xue, perhaps the tomb's occupant or even the brickmaker. What was found were objects the deceased would need in the next life—a stove, pots and pans, a store of grain and other essential items. The custom of burying necessities of life with deceased loved ones continues today, only nowadays videos, cash, servants or a car are deemed must-haves, and they are made out of paper and then burned at funerals and during the month of the Hungry Ghosts (▶ 4).

Lasting image The tomb is sealed and you can see it only by peering through the broken entrance porch. Nonetheless, it remains a potent image of the past that has survived in Hong Kong and you can't help but wonder whether the Hong Kong & Shanghai Banking Corporation building will last as long.

HIGHLIGHTS

- 2,000-year-old Han-dynasty tomb with four side chambers
- Niche at back of chamber for holding funerary urn
- Display room with funerary objects
- Local park, where old men take caged birds for a walk

INFORMATION

- ✛ E2; Locator map B2
- ✉ 41 Tonkin Street, Lei Cheng Uk Estate, Sham Shui Po
- ☎ 2386 2863
- ◐ Mon–Wed, Fri, Sat 10–1, 2–6, Sun 1–6. Closed 25–26 Dec and first three days of the Chinese New Year
- ◉ Cheung Sha Wan
- ▭ 2 from Tonkin Street to Star Ferry
- ♿ Good access to museum displays but not to tomb
- ▨ Free

Statue Square

Statue Square is just one section of a whole chain of pleasant open spaces in the heart of the Central district. The space here allows for amazing views of the towering landmarks of modern architecture all around you.

HIGHLIGHTS

- Hong Kong & Shanghai Banking Corporation Building (➤ 53)
- Old Bank of China Building
- Expatriate Filipino gatherings on Sunday
- By-law signs written in English, Chinese and Togalog
- Statue of Sir Thomas Jackson
- Legislative Council Building
- Cenotaph
- Chater Garden
- Interior of Mandarin Oriental hotel (➤ 86)

INFORMATION

- E8; Locator map F3
- Statue Square, Central
- Central
- Trams to Causeway Bay and Sheung Wan
- Excellent
- Free
- Central Market (➤ 34), Star Ferry (➤ 40)

Colonial core Surrounded by 19th-century buildings this was the heart of colonial Hong Kong Island; its northern edge opened onto the harbor. It is a far cry from that now: its only antique structure is the Legislative Council Building, previously the Supreme Court. The centerpiece was once the statue of Queen Victoria, now in Victoria Park in Causeway Bay.

Surrounding architecture The square today is too built up to qualify as a green area, with its concrete pools and fountains. Much more important is the outstanding architecture around it (➤ 53). Look for Norman Foster's 1986 Hong Kong & Shanghai Banking Corporation Building (walk up to its first floor). Behind and to the east, I. M. Pei's angular 74-story Bank of China Tower (1985–90) lurches

skywards, sending out bad *chi* (➤ 52, panel). More pleasing is the old Bank of China Building (1950), guarded by two fierce stone lions. Between it and the sea is the cenotaph, memorial to the dead of two world wars and of the horrific 1989 Tiananmen Square massacre. On the other side is Chater Garden, once home to the Hong Kong Cricket Club.

Sir Thomas Jackson, merchant banker

Hong Kong Park

In a space-deprived Hong Kong, this modern little park is a joy. Instead of roses or ancient trees you'll find man-made waterfalls, concrete pools and paths around the grass and flowers, all for a sense of harmony and balance.

Artificial paradise Hong Kong Park is a small miracle of artificiality. Its architects used what little original landscape existed and built the park into the contours of the hillside. It's fun to walk past the koi carp-filled pools or through the aviary where tree-high walkways take you cheek by bill with fascinating, brilliantly plumaged tropical birds.

The conservatory The biggest in the world, it contains biospheres maintaining arid, humid and just plain flashy plant environments. The utterly artificial waterfalls are beautifully designed and give a refreshing look and sound. Everywhere the plants are local and indigenous. In particular, the enormous variety of bamboos—from tiny, delicate-stemmed varieties to the huge ones used in scaffolding—are on display.

Refreshments old and new The Museum of Teaware in Flagstaff House, the oldest building in Hong Kong, deserves a whole afternoon. Flagstaff House is a charming piece of mid-19th-century architecture, and the exhibition of teapots and the like brings out the collector in almost everyone. After your visit, you might like to hit the happy hour, which runs between 4 and 7 in the park's bar and restaurant. Most afternoons the park is full of elegantly dressed parties posing for wedding photos, having just emerged from the registry office, which is in the park.

HIGHLIGHTS

- Walk-in aviary
- Artificial waterfalls
- Conservatory
- Flagstaff House and Museum of Teaware
- Observation tower
- *Bonsai* trees in *T'ai Chi* Garden

INFORMATION

- ✚ E8; Locator map F3
- ✉ Main entrancce: Supreme Court Road, Central. Nearest entrance to Museum of Teaware: Cotton Tree Drive, Central
- ☎ Museum: 2869 0690
- 🕐 Park: 6.30am–11pm. Museum: Wed–Mon 10–5. Closed 24–25 Dec, 1 Jan, and first three days of Chinese New Year
- 🍴 Café/bar in park
- Ⓜ Admiralty
- 🚌 12, 23B, 33, 40, 103; get off at first stop in Cotton Tree Drive
- ♿ Good
- 🎫 Free
- ↔ Botanical & Zoological Gardens (► 35)

Star Ferry

HIGHLIGHTS

- Shops in Tsim Sha Tsui ferry terminal
- Vista to east and west along shipping lane
- Hong Kong & Shanghai Banking Corporation Building
- Bank of China Tower
- Convention and Exhibition Centre
- Views of Peak and Mid Levels

INFORMATION

- F7; E8; F8; Locator map E2
- Salisbury Road, Tsim Sha Tsui (Kowloon); Edinburgh Place, Central (Hong Kong Island); Sea Front Road, Wan Chai (Hong Kong Island)
- Hotline: 2367 7065
- Daily 6.30am–11.30pm. Office hours 8.30am–6.30pm
- Small café before Central ferry gate
- Tsim Sha Tsui; Central; Wan Chai
- Main buses from bus stations at the three terminals
- Lower decks more accessible
- Inexpensive
- Central: Exchange Square (► 36), Statue Square (► 38). Tsim Sha Tsui: Space Museum (► 44), Museum of Art (► 45)

The Star Ferry between Kowloon and Hong Kong Island has to be one of the world's most spectacular sea crossings. You get a panoramic view of the harbor as you ply around dredgers, launches and all the other vessels.

Looking back Journey time on the Star Ferry, which has been operating since 1898, is less than ten minutes on a good day, but the views of the cityscape on both sides of the harbor are excellent—and all for HK$12.20. The ferry terminal on the Tsim Sha Tsui side sits beside the incongruous Hong Kong Cultural Centre (1989), with its windowless, smooth-tiled surface (► 53). As the ferry sets off to Hong Kong Island, you can see the long pink and black striped outlines of the Hong Kong Museum of Art (► 45).

Looking forward Ahead, on the island itself, the stunning architecture of the reclaimed shoreline spike the sky, dominated by the Convention and Exhibition Centre, which opened in 1988, with its twin towers of New World Harbour View and Hyatt hotels. It was built in two phases, the first by architects Mr Ng Chun & Associates, the second by Wong & Ouyang. Behind it is Central Plaza, at 78 floors Hong Kong's tallest office building (► 52). West of these buildings are the General Post Office and the striped towers of the Stock Exchange, built by Remo Riva in 1986. Behind these are the Hong Kong & Shanghai Banking Corporation Building (► 53), all glass and innards, and Pei's controversial Bank of China Tower (► 52). Try to pinpoint the various towers, each one competing with the others for advertising space, harbor views and a position in the *Guinness Book of Records*.

Museum of History

This gem of a Hong Kong history museum, both user-friendly and informative, is a good place to spend an hour or two, especially as the curators frequently introduce new touring shows and exhibits.

Exhibits The museum, set in the park, does an excellent job of turning what might be a dry set of historical records into an understandable account of the lives of the people who have inhabited Hong Kong over the years. There is a model sampan to peer into, the interior of a modest Hakka home, and costumes of the peoples who migrated south from China into the New Territories. Of more recent vintage is the full-scale replica of a street in the city of Victoria, as Central was once known. The exhibits are fascinating, especially the entire medicine shop that was moved from its original site in Wan Chai. Other façades in the 19th-century street are of a pawn shop, opium den, print shop, teahouse and a shop selling dried fish. Still other exhibits explore the burgeoning Hong Kong manufacturing industry of the 1950s, which produced cheap enamelware and tin toys for the world's children.

The photographic collection Even more telling are the photographs in the museum; some are of the plague that hit Hong Kong in the late 19th century, others show daily life in the streets of Hong Kong, and several much later photographs illustrate the effects the worst typhoons and landslides have had on the territory.

HIGHLIGHTS

- Early photographs
- Full-size replica of sampan
- Herbalist shop
- Interior of Eurasian family home
- *Chai mun* (ornamental plank) from temple
- Kowloon Park

INFORMATION

- ✚ F6; Locator map D2
- ✉ 100 Chatham Road South, Tsim Sha Tsui
- ☎ 2724 9042
- 🕐 Mon–Wed 10–6, Sun and public holidays 10–7
- 🚇 Tsim Sha Tsui
- ♿ Excellent
- 🎟 Inexpensive
- ↔ Space Museum (► 44), Museum of Art (► 45)
- ❓ Audiovisual shows. Free guided tours in English Sat, Sun 10.30, 2.30

Queen's Road c1915

Ocean Park

HIGHLIGHTS

- Atoll reef aquarium
- Shark aquarium
- Ocean Theatre animal shows
- Raging River flume ride
- Aviary
- Bird shows
- Dragon Ride

INFORMATION

www.oceanpark.com.hk

- Off map to south; Locator map C2
- Aberdeen, Hong Kong
- 2552 0291
- Daily 10–6
- Several fast-food eateries inside
- Ocean Park Citibus leaves from Exchange Square Bus Terminus every half hour
- Excellent Expensive
- Height restrictions on some rides

Dolphin ride

Wildlife, history, scenic views, arts and crafts and animal shows—not to mention thrilling rides—make up this park. It's a whole day's entertainment—and a jam-packed day at that.

Thrills galore There is so much to see and do at this park that it takes a little doing to figure out a plan. So start by finding out the times and locations of the animal shows; then plan the rest of your day around them. The rides really are stomach-turning, the creatures in the aquarium scary, and the animal and plant exhibits well-displayed and well-maintained. Don't miss the Raging River breathtaking flume ride.

Aerial view Most fun of all, perhaps, is the cable-car trip into the place. You dangle in a fragile little car, stopping and starting for no apparent reason as the wind whistles around and under you, with the sea gently boiling below. And to come out of the park you take a four-section, 745-ft (227-m) long escalator ride. Try to avoid weekends, when the place gets very crowded, and note there are minimum height restrictions on some rides.

Temple Street

At about 7pm each night, stalls sprout on either side of this street and are hung with T-shirts, lingerie, jeans and other goodies. Earlier in the day, stalls do a brisk trade in jade.

After dark The market is full of bargains in silk shirts, leather items and bric-a-brac, as well as jeans and T-shirts. Nothing on sale is really indigenous as locals rather than the visitors are the buyers. After about 7.30pm the street is closed to traffic, and at the crossroads in the middle of the market, two fresh-fish restaurants set up their tables. Their counters, also out in the street, contain all manner of wriggling things that you can pick out to be cooked for your dinner.

Jade for sale At the end of the street, near the junction of Battery and Kansu streets under a flyover, is the jade market. Here, until they close up at about 3pm, hundreds of stalls sell all kinds of jade, which comes in many shades besides green—from white through to purple. Locals spend the afternoon bargaining over prices, which range from inexpensive to a king's ransom. Unless you know what you are doing this is not the place for a major investment.

Still more stalls In adjoining streets are vegetable and fruit stalls, shops selling fabrics and traditional red-embroidered Chinese wedding outfits and many Chinese medicine shops. If you are lucky, you may catch a Chinese opera performance, sung in Cantonese, on a makeshift stage of bamboo and canvas.

Tradition As you walk through the market, look for people playing the age-old game of mahjong in the backs of shops or set up in corners.

HIGHLIGHTS

- Fresh fish set out on stalls
- Fortune-tellers
- Chinese medicine shops
- Shops selling traditional Chinese wedding clothes
- Jade market
- Yau Ma Tei Typhoon Shelter, to the west
- Racks of T-shirts
- Exotic vegetables in vegetable market

INFORMATION

- ✚ F5–6; Locator map off D2
- ✉ Temple Street, Kansu Street, Reclamation Street, Kowloon
- 🕐 Jade market: 10–4. Temple Street market: 8am–11pm. Vegetable market: early morning and early evening
- 🍴 Seafood restaurants and hawker center in Temple Street
- 🚇 Jordan
- ♿ Good
- 💷 Free
- ↔ Lei Cheng Uk Museum (▶ 37)

Space Museum

HIGHLIGHTS

- Omnimax Theatre
- *Mercury* space capsule
- Hall of Space Science
- Solar telescope
- Planetarium show
- Hall of Astronomy

INFORMATION

- F7; Locator map D2
- 10 Salisbury Road (next to the Hong Kong Cultural Centre, Tsim Sha Tsui
- 2721 0226
- Mon, Wed–Fri 1–8 (Fri 9.45pm), Sat, Sun 10–9
- Tsim Sha Tsui
- Tsim Sha Tsui bus station
- Star Ferry to Central and Wan Chai
- Excellent Expensive
- Hong Kong Science Museum (▶ 60)
- Children under three are not allowed in the Omnimax

This museum, which has one of the world's largest and most advanced planetariums, is fascinating for kids, with plenty of hands-on exhibits, a *Mercury* space capsule, and daily Omnimax and Space Theatre shows.

Layout and Omnimax The museum's oval, pink building, built in 1980 by the Architectural Services Department, is in itself stunning. Inside are three exhibitions: the Hall of Astronomy, the Hall of Space Science and the most popular, the Omnimax Theatre. If you haven't seen an Omnimax film before, then seize the chance here. You sit back in tilted seats and gaze ahead and up at a screen that covers most of the ceiling and front wall. If you get at all queasy at thrill rides at amusement parks, close your eyes during the parts where someone jumps out of an aeroplane or travels around in a roller coaster—these are very realistic.

Exhibition halls The Space Science Exhibition includes bits of moon rock, manned spaced flight, the actual *Mercury* space capsule piloted by Scott Carpenter in 1962, future space programs, and plenty more. In the Museum of Astronomy there is a solar telescope where you can look directly at the sun. Did you know that it was ancient Chinese astronomers who were the first to spot Halley's Comet and the first to chart the movements of the stars?

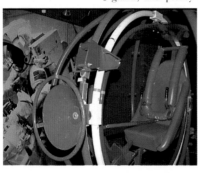

Gravity chair, with astronaut in action shown behind

Museum of Art

A beautifully laid-out series of galleries contain displays of exquisite Chinese calligraphy and painting, both traditional and modern, many stunning ancient artifacts and a collection of jade, ivory and pottery.

Chinese antiquities Opened in 1989, next door to the Hong Kong Cultural Centre complex, the museum has seven galleries, four containing Chinese antiquities, local artists' work and pictures of historical note as well as artistic worth. The thousands of exhibits in the Chinese antiquities section range from rhino-horn cups to burial goods and lavish tomb adornments; of particular interest are two large Tang dynasty (AD618–906) tomb guardians in the form of mythical beasts. The jade and ivory carvings in the Decorative Arts gallery are especially lovely.

Art galleries The best gallery is the one containing old pictures and prints of Hong Kong. It is hard to believe that the sandy beaches and jungle-filled hills could have become such a different kind of jungle in so short a space of time. The painting of the city of Victoria (as the built-up part of Hong Kong was called) is a revelation of just how far the colony has come since the early 19th century.

Modern art The works in the contemporary art gallery are divided into decades, and it is particularly interesting to see the development of local art since the 1950s. There is also a collection of calligraphy and Chinese paintings, and a special gallery for international exhibitions. Between galleries, leather armchairs facing the enormous corridor windows allow you to enjoy the wonderful waterfront vista.

HIGHLIGHTS

- Han-dynasty pottery watchtower
- Tang-dynasty tomb guardians
- Translucent rhino-horn cups
- Description of Quing kiln
- Painting of city of Victoria (1854)
- Painting of Wyndham Street
- *The Baptism* in contemporary art gallery
- Models of merchant boats and sea-going junk
- Model of Guangzhou
- Lithograph of Hong Kong Harbour

INFORMATION

- F7; Locator map E2
- 10 Sailsbury Road (next door to the Hong Kong Cultural Centre), Tsim Sha Tsui
- 2721 0116
- Fri–Wed 10–6. Closed some public holidays
- Museum café
- Tsim Sha Tsui
- Tsim Sha Tsui bus station
- Star Ferry to Wan Chai and Central
- Excellent
- Expensive
- Star Ferry (➤ 40)
- Museum bookshop

A Symphony of Lights

HIGHLIGHTS

- Harbor trip
- The cool of the Tsim Sha Tsui promenade
- Occasional pyrotechnic additions to the show
- The view beyond the harborfront to the Peak

INFORMATION

- F7; Locator map E2
- 8pm–8.18pm
- Tsim Sha Tsui
- Good
- Free
- Harbor cruises with the Star Ferry; www.star ferry.com.hk

Victoria Harbour has to be one of the most amazing sights of a trip to Hong Kong. Each evening a stunning light and sound show takes place creating a vibrant frenzy along the waterfront.

Dazzling display Impressive though it has always been, Victoria Harbour is even more striking since the introduction of "A Symphony of Lights." It is a stirring experience to stand and watch this 18-minute performance by the buildings along the waterfront on Hong Kong Island. Every day at 8pm the exteriors of 18 of the city's major buildings glow with a myriad of vivid colors with the use of a wide range of architectural lights to draw the eye along the waterfront. Best viewed from Tsim Sha Tsui, one building after another lights up, highlighting its outline or changing its appearance altogether. A narration and music are broadcast each night (in English on Monday, Wednesday and Friday) along the Avenue of Stars, while onlookers from Tsim Sha Tsui can tune into the narration by radio (English channel available). On certain special occasions the light display is complemented by rooftop pyrotechnic displays on some buildings. You can also take one of the harbor cruises and listen to the narration and music piped aboard.

Take an evening stroll The walk along the promenade in Tsim Sha Tsui from the Cultural Centre eastwards is a lovely experience in itself. Often quite empty or dotted with courting couples and old men fishing the walk, makes a cool, relaxing end to a hectic Hong Kong day. The Avenue of Stars has been launched along the promenade with handprint plaques commemorating the icons of the Hong Kong film industry.

Lighting up the night sky in Victoria Harbour

Ten Thousand Buddhas Temple

A half-hour train ride out of Hong Kong brings you to this striking temple set on a hillside overlooking the apartments, housing projects and towers of the satellite town of Sha Tin.

Bountiful Buddhas To reach the temple, take the train to Sha Tin and follow the signs. You must then climb 431 steps up the hillside. Known locally as Man Fat Sze Temple, this Buddhist shrine has, since it was built in the 1950s, become known as the Ten Thousand Buddhas Temple because of the many small statues that decorate it, the donations of grateful worshippers over the years. The statues are all different—some black, some covered in gold leaf—and each Buddha strikes a different pose.

Panoramas and pagodas From the edge of the courtyard there are magnificent views over Sha Tin. The courtyard houses a tiered pagoda and the statues of some of Buddha's followers. Higher up is another set of four temples, one containing Hong Kong's second-tallest Buddha statue, another the embalmed, gilded remains of Yuet Kai, who founded the Man Fat Sze monastery.

HIGHLIGHTS

- Thousands of small statues of Buddha
- Tallest-standing Buddha statue in Hong Kong
- Embalmed and gilded body of monastery's founder
- Statues of Buddha's followers
- Views over Sha Tin
- 400-odd steps up to monastery
- Views of Amah Rock

INFORMATION

- ✚ Off map to north; Locator map A2
- ✉ Close to Pai Tau Street, Sha Tin, New Territories
- 🕐 Daily 8–6. Particularly busy around Chinese New Year
- 🚇 Sha Tin
- ♿ None
- 🎫 Free, but donations welcome

Courtyard of the Ten Thousand Buddhas Temple

Wong Tai Sin Temple

If temples were shops, then Wong Tai Sin Temple would be a supermarket. During Chinese New Year, you risk having your hair set on fire by hundreds of devotees waving joss sticks as they whirl from one deity to the next.

Wong Tai Sin This large Taoist temple, built in 1973 in Chinese style and situated among high-rise residential blocks, is dedicated to Wong Tai Sin, an ex-shepherd who was taught how to cure all ills by a passing deity. In modern-day Hong Kong, Wong Tai Sin is a very popular god, as he is in charge of the fortunes of gamblers. He can also be sought out by those who are ill or who have concerns about their health, and by people asking for help in business matters.

Symbolic interior The temple complex is vast, almost stadium-sized, composed not just of the main temple, where Wong Tai Sin is represented by a painting rather than a statue, but also by turtle ponds, libraries, medicine halls and what is almost a small shopping mall of fortunetellers. The temple is built to represent the geomantic elements of gold, wood, water, fire and earth. In the Yue Heung Shrine are fire and earth; gold is represented in the Bronze Luen Pavilion where the portrait of Wong Tai Sin is kept; and the Library Hall and water fountain represent wood and water respectively.

Philosophy The temple also caters to those who venerate Confucius, represented in the Confucius Hall, while Buddhists come here to worship the Buddhist goddess of mercy, Kuan Yin, in the Three Saints Hall alongside Kwan Ti, and the eight immortals.

HIGHLIGHTS

- Main altar including painting of Wong Tai Sin
- Garden of Nine Dragon Wall
- Fortune-telling arcade
- Clinic Block
- Stalls outside selling windmills and hell money
- Chinese gardens at rear of complex
- Side altar in main temple dedicated to monkey god
- Incinerators for burning offerings

INFORMATION

- H1; Locator map B2
- Wong Tai Sin Estate; follow signs from MTR station
- Information hotline: 2854 4333
- Daily 7–5. Main temple is not always accessible
- Wong Tai Sin
- Good
- Free, but donations welcome

Kowloon Walled City Park

Once the most notorious, lawless and poverty stricken place in Hong Kong, Kowloon Walled City is now a finely manicured park, filled with pavilions, topiary and shady walks. Even the shrubs have been cut and shaped into animal figures.

From ruin to park In 1898 when Britain leased the New Territories from China, Kowloon Walled City was a Chinese garrison and was never included in any agreement. The two countries bickered over its jurisdiction for almost 100 years while the place became ever more ramshackle, with blocks of tenements raised without any kind of planning, non-existent sanitation and frequent outbreaks of disease. During World War II the Japanese knocked the actual walls down to extend the old Kai Tak airport and thousands of illegal immigrants from China found a post-war refuge there. The two governments finally reached a settlement over the area in 1987, the 30,000 inhabitants were rehoused and the buildings were flattened, archaeologists rummaged around and finally a park was built in the ruins. The park is complete with pagodas, a Chinese zodiac garden, a mountain view pavilion and a hill-top pavilion.

Historic survivor For all the years of squalor one of the original buildings of the fort survived and has been restored. It is the Yamen, the administrative building of the assistant magistrate of Kowloon and dates back to the early days of the fort in the 19th century. The three-halled building now holds a display of photos and other items concerning the history of the walled city. Also discovered in the clearance of the buildings were the stone plaques which marked the south gate of the walled city.

HIGHLIGHTS

- Pretty, quiet space in the middle of Kowloon
- Turtle and goldfish ponds
- Artistic topiary
- Renovated administrative building

INFORMATION

- H2; Locator map B2
- Junction of Tung Tau Tsuen and Tung Tsing roads, Kowloon
- Daily 6am–11.30pm
- Lok Fu
- Good
- Free

Stanley

HIGHLIGHTS

- Views from bus to Stanley
- Tin Hau Temple
- Stanley Beach
- St. Stephen's Beach
- Stanley Military Cemetery
- Stanley market
- Kuan Yin Temple

INFORMATION

- Off map to south; Locator map C2
- Market: 10.30–9. Temple: 6–6
- Restaurants and pub food in Stanley Main Street
- 6, 260 from Central Bus Terminus
- Excellent

The most stunning thing about a visit to Stanley, in the south of Hong Kong Island, is the scenic and at times precarious journey there. Get an upstairs seat on the double-decker bus—the ride is as good as any at Ocean Park.

Temples Most visitors come to Stanley Village for its market, but it has many other attractions. Close to the market is the Tin Hau Temple, first built on this spot in the early 1700s. The bell and drum are said to have belonged to a famous pirate, Cheung Po-Tsai. The bell was cast in 1767, and it is thought that the pirate used it to send messages to his ships. The temple also contains the skin of a tiger, shot in Stanley in 1942. During the Japanese invasion the villagers took refuge inside the temple, and although the building was hit twice, neither bomb exploded. Farther along the road is a second temple, dedicated to Kuan Yin, the goddess of mercy. Claims have been made that the 20-ft (6-m) statue of the goddess has moved. Nowadays Stanley is a commuter town, popular with expatriate workers.

Beaches and the market The beach at Stanley is a good one, and a short bus ride farther along takes you to St. Stephen's Beach, where there is a graveyard for all the soldiers who have died in Hong Kong since Britain claimed the island as a colony. Although now rather touristy, the famous market is quite good, with linen shops as well as stalls selling clothes made in other Asian countries.

Stanley market

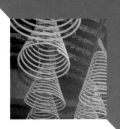

HONG KONG's
best

Architecture *52–53*

Green Spaces *54*

Temples *55*

Markets *56–57*

Shopping Malls *58–59*

For Kids *60*

What's Free *61*

Journeys *62*

Architecture

Bank of China Tower

GEOMANCERS

Almost all building that goes on in Hong Kong is overseen by a *feng shui* (literally "wind and water") master, someone who knows how the life force, or *chi*, moves around the planet's surface. Sharp angles send out bad *chi*, while strategically placed water and mirrors can enhance good *chi* by allowing it to flow smoothly and not get trapped in corners. The master may have much to say about the building's structure; he also studies the site and will decide an auspicious day for starting work.

In the Top 25
🔟 EXCHANGE SQUARE (► 36)

BANK OF CHINA TOWER

Designed by the Chinese-American architect, I. M. Pei and built between 1985 and 1990, this 984-ft (300-m) high, 70-floor tower dominates the Hong Kong skyline. The building soars upwards in a series of triangles towards a prism at the top. Amazingly, it is built with no internal supporting columns. The entrance hall has barrelled vaults in the style of a Ming dynasty tomb—a mixture of the ultramodern and the historic. It is world famous for its bad *chi* owing to the use of sharp angles creating a sinister shape.

➕ E8 ✉ No. 1 Garden Road, Central 🕐 Mon–Fri 8–6
🚇 Central 🎟 Free

CENTRAL PLAZA

Completed in 1992, Central Plaza was, for a few years Hong Kong's tallest building at 78 floors and 1,227ft (374m)—counting the spire. Majestic both inside and out, it incorporates a huge public space, in the form of a piazza at ground level and a through walkway on the first level. The whole mood is one of brooding neoclassical grandeur, with its vast lobby containing huge palm trees and some terrific artwork. The architects were Dennis Lau and Ng Chun Man.

➕ F8 ✉ Harbour Road, Wan Chai 🚇 Wan Chai 🎟 Free

HONG KONG & SHANGHAI BANKING CORPORATION BUILDING

This 1985 building, designed by Britain's Sir Norman Foster and prefabricated in several different continents at a cost of over US$1 billion, looks as if it's been turned inside out. The supporting structures appear on the outside, all mechanical parts are exposed, and many walls are glass. A geomancer decided the alignment and angles of the escalators.

✚ E8 ⊠ Des Voeux Road/Statue Square, Central 🚇 Central 🎟 Free

HONG KONG CONVENTION & EXHIBITION CENTRE

Built on reclaimed land and opened in 1988, this massive complex looks bland when approached from the harbor, despite the fact that its towers contain two of the island's most prestigious hotels—the Grand Hyatt and the Renaissance Harbour View—plus some 19,375sq ft (1,800sq m) of exhibition space. On the harbor side of the exhibition hall is a seven-floor plate-glass window. Escalators go alongside it up to the seventh floor, giving great harbor views.

✚ F8 ⊠ 1 Convention Avenue, Wan Chai ☎ 2582 8888 🚇 Wan Chai 🎟 Free

HONG KONG CULTURAL CENTRE

Designed by the government's architectural services department in 1989, this is one of Hong Kong's most controversial buildings. It has a huge sloping roof that is matched by the dome of the nearby Space Museum, and is uniformly pink. The building is also windowless—rather odd as it would have one of the most dynamic views in the world. Inside, it is all very modern, especially the sparse auditoriums with their apparently unsupported balconies. At the rear is a waterfront walkway.

✚ F7 ⊠ Salisbury Road, Tsim Sha Tsui ☎ 2734 2009 🚇 Tsim Sha Tsui 🎟 Free

INTERNATIONAL FINANCE CENTRE

Intended to inject new life into Hong Kong's position as the financial center of Asia, this building and its next door neighbour are impressive, if not as stunning as other buildings in the area. No. 2, designed by Cesar Pelli, the architect of London's Canary Wharf, soars 88 floors into the sky along simple lines. The two towers of vast office space, sit on what will be a massive shopping, entertainment and hotel complex.

✚ D8 ⊠ 1, Harbour View, Central 🚇 Central 🎟 Free

Hong Kong Convention & Exhibition Centre

FENG SHUI IN PRACTICE

When the Conrad Hotel was redesigned in 1997, coins were buried beneath the floor of the downstairs lobby, itself in the shape of a Chinese coin. The carp and lily paintings on the walls of the hotel lobby represent pools of water, so bring in good *chi* and hold it there. At the Excelsior Hotel, built in 1973, the Chinese restaurant was designed with temporary moving partitions so that the series of small rooms could periodically be opened up into a large loop, allowing a good flow of *chi* through the restaurant.

Green Spaces

┌─ In the Top 25 ─────────────────────┐
5 CHE KEI SHAN (VICTORIA PEAK) (▶ 30)
14 HONG KONG PARK (▶ 39)
24 KOWLOON WALLED CITY PARK (▶ 49)
└──────────────────────────────────────┘

CHEUNG CHAU

Cheung Chau has two good beaches, lots of seafood restaurants, some interesting temples, caves, windsurfing equipment and bicycles for rent, good walks, no traffic and an annual bun festival.
🕐 Hourly ferries start around 6.30pm. Last ferry returns around 11.45pm 🚢 Outlying Islands Pier, Central 💷 Moderate

Cheung Chau Island

KOWLOON PARK (▶ 61)

LAMMA ISLAND

Great beaches, good seafood restaurants, places to walk and no cars. Even the power station and a huge quarry do not spoil your day. Best beach—Mo Tat Wan.
🕐 Ferries run approx 7am–10.30pm 🚢 Outlying Islands Pier, Central 💷 Moderate; double on weekends

COUNTRY PARKS

Hong Kong Island has five country parks, areas of protected countryside, all linked together along the 31-mile (50-km) Hong Kong Trail, a well-laid out footpath. Each park has barbecue sites and other facilities, but they do get very crowded on weekends. However, if you venture any distance along the trail you soon leave the crowds behind. The most accessible park is probably Pok Fu Lam Country Park, which can be reached on foot from the Peak or by the No. 15 bus from Central.

SAI KUNG PENINSULA

This is the green lung of Hong Kong, containing the 18,772-acre (7,600-ha) Ma On Shan Country Park, a reservoir, the Maclehose walking trail, a marine park and the fourth highest peak in the territory. Start off at Sai Kung village, go island hopping, wind surfing or walk the trails around the park.
➕ L1–N1 (country park); locator map A2 (peninsula) 🕐 Visitor center 9.30–4.30 🚇 KCR to Sha Tin then bus 299 to Sai Kung village

TAI TAM COUNTRY PARK

An excellent country park to get away from it all. You can walk along the coast and around a reservoir, past World War II bunkers and fortified gun emplacements. Bring sturdy shoes and plenty of drinking water.
➕ J8–K8/9/10 🚇 Wan Chai MTR, then minibus 16M or 🚌 6 from Exchange Square to Hong Kong Cricket Club, then walk past petrol station and take first left up steps

VICTORIA PARK

This relatively enormous patch of green is used to its limits, including its sports pitches, pool and pleasant green walks. Early morning *t'ai chi ch'uan* takes place and many events are staged here.
➕ G8–H8 ✉ Causeway Bay, Hong Kong Island 🚋 Tram from Wan Chai or Central (look for one labeled "Causeway Bay") 💷 Free

Temples

┌─ **In the Top 25**
│ 🏯 **KUAN YIN TEMPLE, STANLEY (▶ 50)**
│ 🏯 **MAN MO TEMPLE (▶ 33)**
│ 🏯 **TIN HAU TEMPLE, STANLEY (▶ 50)**
│ 🏯 **WONG TAI SIN TEMPLE (▶ 48)**

LU PAN TEMPLE

Usually empty and quiet, this is the only temple in Hong Kong dedicated to Lu Pan, the master builder who repaired the pillars of heaven. His festival is celebrated by construction workers. The temple has elaborate roof ceramics and carvings above the door.

➕ B8   ✉ Li Po Lung Path, off Belcher's Street, Kennedy Town
🕐 Daily 8–7   🚌 3 from Rumsey Steet, Central   💵 Free

MAN MO TEMPLE, TAI PO (▶ 20)

HUNG SHENG TEMPLE

This temple, built quite a way back into the rock-face behind it, is dedicated to the scholar Hung Sheng, who was able to foretell the weather. Several elderly fortune-tellers have set up little shrines around it.

➕ F9   ✉ 131 Queen's Road East, Wan Chai   🕐 Daily 8–6
🚇 Wan Chai   💵 Free

TIN HAU TEMPLE, CAUSEWAY BAY

Dedicated to Tin Hau, the goddess who protects seafarers, this is one of many temples scattered along Hong Kong's coastline. The temple, perched on a rock above the road, is about 200 years old, although it has been renovated.

➕ H8   ✉ Tin Hau Street, Causeway Bay   🕐 Daily 7–5   🚇 Tin Hau
💵 Free

TIN HAU TEMPLE, KOWLOON

Kowloon's temple of the goddess of the sea and seafarers, after which Temple Street is named, is one of Kowloon's oldest. Once it looked out to the sea, now several blocks away.

➕ F5   ✉ Market Street, Kowloon   🕐 Daily 8–6   🚇 Jordan
💵 Free

TIN HAU TEMPLE, REPULSE BAY

Yet another Tin Hau temple dedicated to the goddess of fisherfolk, this one has a longevity bridge in front of it. The legend goes that crossing it add three years to your life.

✉ Repulse Bay Beach   🕐 Daily 8–6   🚌 6, 61 from
Central Bus Terminus   💵 Free

OTHER PLACES OF WORSHIP

Many religions are practiced in Hong Kong beside Taoism and Buddhism. The colony has a synagogue and two mosques as well as many churches. The two most prominent are the Roman Catholic cathedral, built in 1880 by Portuguese Catholics from Macau, and the Anglican St. John's Cathedral in Garden Road, built in 1847. Both are open to the public and well worth a visit, if only for the sense of what life must have been like in 19th-century Hong Kong.

Roof decoration of Wong Tai Sin Temple

Markets

BIRD MARKETS

Songbirds have always played an important part in Hong Kong's social life. Keeping the birds is a male activity, and an elderly man taking his bird for a walk is a common sight in parks. There are regular impromptu bird-song competitions, when a judge listens to the songs of birds in different cages, and large sums of money are wagered on which bird will win the prize. The bird cages are little works of art in themselves, often carved out of mahogany or bamboo.

In the Top 25

🔟 **JADE MARKET** (► 43)
🔟 **STANLEY MARKET** (► 50)
🔟 **TEMPLE STREET NIGHT MARKET** (► 43)

APLIU STREET

Tour buses rarely include this thoroughly Chinese market area in their itineraries. It sells clothes, inexpensive CDs and sundry items. The Golden Shopping Centre (► 75) is in the vicinity.
➕ E3 ✉ Apliu Street, Sham Shui Po, Kowloon 🕒 Daily mid-morning to late 🚇 Sham Shui Po

BIRD MARKET

This market is dedicated to the sale of songbirds and all the associated paraphernalia, from bird seed to cages. Local bird fanciers prefer the tiny birds, but you will also find more exotic creatures such as parrots and mynahs. Look for cages of crickets, which are fed to the birds with chopsticks.
➕ F3 ✉ Yuen Po Street, Mong Kok 🕒 Daily 7am–8pm
🚇 Mong Kok

Bird market

FA YUEN STREET

Two blocks heaving with local life There are some amazing bargains in inexpensive clothes.
➕ F3 ✉ Prince Edward MTR 🕒 Daily 10am–late

FLOWER MARKET

A whole street is given over to potted-plant and

cut-flower stalls. Look for the carnivorous pitcher plants and beautiful but very expensive bonsai. Silk flowers are also sold.

🔲 F3 ✉ Flower Market Road, Kowloon 🕐 Daily 9–6
🚇 Prince Edward

Card players near Jade Market

JARDINE'S BAZAAR

This is one of Hong Kong's oldest street markets, full of food shops, good shops selling clothes and handbags, and excellent bargains in inexpensive clothes.

🔲 G8 ✉ Jardine's Bazaar and Jardine's Crescent, Causeway Bay
🕐 Daily mid-morning to late 🚇 Causeway Bay

LADIES' MARKET

This market easily rivals Temple Street, and although once solely dedicated to women's clothes, it now has bargains for everyone, including printed T-shirts, belts, inexpensive jeans and watches. It covers about four blocks of densest Mong Kok, so you have to love crowds to shop here.

🔲 F4 ✉ Tung Choi Street, Mong Kok 🕐 Daily noon–10
🚇 Mong Kok

LI YUEN STREET EAST AND WEST

A clothes, handbag, fabric and accessories market, one of Hong Kong's oldest, with some excellent bargains, particularly in leather goods. It could be combined with the factory outlets in the Pedder Building (► 79).

🔲 D8 ✉ Off Queen's Road Central, Central 🕐 Daily noon–late
🚇 Central

MARBLE ROAD MARKET

This busy working local market sells fresh produce and there are bargains in T-shirts and clothes. A fish market is nearby.

🔲 J7 ✉ Marble Road, North Point 🕐 Daily noon–late 🚋 Tram from Causeway Bay, Wan Chai or Central

UPPER LASCAR ROW

A flea market set alongside more expensive shops and selling the same kind of bric-a-brac, records and curios, along with the occasional antique.

🔲 D8 ✉ Off Queen's Road West, Sheung Wan 🕐 Daily 11–6
🚇 Sheung Wan

WESTERN MARKET

Gift items, crafts, paintings, fabrics and restaurants.

🔲 D7 ✉ New Market Street, Sheung Wan 🕐 Daily 10 –7
🚇 Sheung Wan

FLOWER MARKETS

Hong Kong's several markets dedicated to flowers sell mostly cut flowers and silk ones. Around Chinese New Year additional flower markets spring up all around—a particularly big one is held in Victoria Park. Families go there to buy kumquat trees, orange trees and plum-blossom branches to decorate their homes. Particularly popular at this time are exquisitely perfumed daffodils and gladioli.

Shopping Malls

PACIFIC PLACE

Pacific Place is part of a vast linked chain of shopping malls that spreads out around Admiralty MTR station. Built around a very tall atrium, decorated in granite pink, chrome and glass, it is visually captivating as well as a great place to shop. Most shops sell clothes, but you will also find three hotels, restaurants, fast-food joints, a huge branch of Marks & Spencer, a supermarket, three cinemas and a Seibu Japanese department store. The main concourse is often the venue for free concerts.

Admiralty Building

CHATER HOUSE

Hong Kong's newest temple to retail outlets, Chater House is huge, with lots of big names to match, including an Armani mega-store. With its slick escalators this is a very exclusive place to be.

🚇 D8 ✉ 11 Chater Road ⏰ Daily 9–8 🚇 Central

CITYPLAZA I AND II

Try this if you want to see one that is used by lots of locals and is rarely visited by tourists. It has shops with fixed prices, and its two skating rinks—roller and ice—have attracted childrenswear and toy stores. Also men's and women's clothes shops.

🚇 K8 ✉ 1111 King's Road, Taikoo Shing ⏰ Daily 9–8 🚇 Tai Koo

IFC MALL

Over 200 international brand names, good restaurants, cinemas and the Airport Express all in a harborside location.

🚇 D8 ✉ 1 Harbour View Street ⏰ Daily 9–8 🚇 Central

THE LANDMARK

A very exclusive mall with all the big-name designer labels and prices to match. There are numerous cafés and a huge atrium with an impressive fountain, where free concerts are frequently given. Another attraction is the musical clock, decorated with figures from the Chinese zodiac.

🚇 D8 ✉ Des Voeux Road and Pedder Street, Central ⏰ Daily 9–8 🚇 Central

NEW WORLD CENTRE

Slightly more elegant and rarefied than the other malls, but a bit gloomy and architecturally unimpressive, the New World Centre has lots of shops selling silks and jade, as well as some excellent rosewood and lacquer furniture shops.

🚇 F7 ✉ Salisbury Road, Tsim Sha Tsui ⏰ Daily 9–8 🚇 Tsim Sha Tsui

OCEAN TERMINAL

This mega mall stretches along the length of Canton Road and seems to go on forever. It has a wide variety of shops ranging from designer fashion to interesting furniture and fabric shops.

🚇 F6 ✉ Canton Road, Tsim Sha Tsui ⏰ Daily 9–8 🚇 Tsim Sha Tsui

Pacific Place

PACIFIC PLACE

You could live and die in this shopping mall without ever having to leave. (► panel opposite). The ultimate in shopping complexes.

➕ E8   ✉ 88 Queensway, Central   🕐 Daily 9–8   🚇 Admiralty

SHUN TAK CENTRE

The biggest mall in the western end of the island, this is built around a residential hotel, offices and the ferry terminal to Macau. It has large open spaces with cafés, food stalls, lots of local chain stores and some interesting clothes and leather shops. Worth popping into on a trip to Western Market—it's almost directly opposite—for its air-conditioning and refreshments as well as the shops.

➕ D7   ✉ 200 Connaught Road, Sheung Wan   🕐 Daily 9–8   🚇 Sheung Wan

TIMES SQUARE

This is the center that changed the landscape of Causeway Bay when it was built in 1999. In this space-age super mall, each of 12 floors is dedicated to a certain type of product—all the computer merchandise is on one floor, the women's clothes are on another, and so on. There are over 200 shops within the complex. It is in the excellent shopping area of Causeway Bay, with other plazas close by as well as several Japanese department stores and Chinese products shops, so if you have time to visit only one shopping area choose this one. Stay away on weekends, when vast crowds flood in.

➕ G8   ✉ Matheson Street, Causeway Bay   🕐 Daily 9–8   🚇 Causeway Bay

HARBOUR CITY

The Harbour City complex in Tsim Sha Tsui is one of the world's longest shopping complexes and includes Ocean Centre, Ocean Galleries, a few hotels and Ocean Terminal. If you can't find what you want here, it probably doesn't exist.

For Children

┌─ **In the Top 25** ─────────
₁₇ OCEAN PARK (► 42)

CITY PLAZA II ICE PALACE

This shopping complex houses an ice-skating rink where the admission price covers a morning or afternoon session as well as skate rental. Close by is Roller Rabbit roller-skating rink and a ten-pin bowling alley, Fourseas.

➕ K8 ✉ Tai Koo Shing, Hong Kong Island 🍴 Cafés 🚇 Tai Koo Shing

Ice Palace: ☎ 2885 6697 🕐 Daily 7am–10pm 💷 Moderate
Fourseas Bowling Centre: ☎ 2567 0763 🕐 Daily 9.30am–1am
💷 Moderate

DRAGON SHOPPING CENTRE

The main attraction of this shopping complex, opened in 1996, is the rollercoaster ride that whizzes about inside the building. There is also a skating rink and a video arcade. You can get in some serious shopping while the kids have fun.

➕ E2 ✉ Yen Chow Street, Sham Shui Po ☎ 2360 0982
🕐 Daily 11–10 🚇 Sham Shui Po MTR 💷 Ride: inexpensive

HONG KONG SCIENCE MUSEUM

In this multilevel hands-on museum kids and science freaks will definitely get a kick out of the zany, yet eductional, interactive exhibits on permanent display—some 500 in all, covering computers, robotics, energy, physics, transportation, communications and much more. Over half of the total exhibits are interactive.

➕ F6 ✉ 2 Science Museum Road, Tsim Sha Tsui ☎ 2732 3231
🕐 Tue–Fri 1–9, Sat, Sun 10–9 🚌 6 from Hanlow Road or taxi from Tsim Sha Tsui MTR 💷 Moderate

POK FU LAM PUBLIC RIDING SCHOOL

This riding school on the southwest of the Island provides lessons for all abilities. Be sure to telephone in advance.

➕ C10 ✉ 75 Reservoir Road, Pok Fu Lam
☎ 2550 1359 🕐 Sep–end of Jun Tue–Sun
💷 Moderate

POLICE MUSEUM (► 61)

REPULSE BAY

The pretty beach here gets very crowded on public holidays and on weekends, but there is a temple (► 55) and a modern shopping arcade to visit when the heat gets too much.

🚌 6, 61 from Central Bus Terminus 💷 Free

MORE IDEAS

Like the rest of us, children enjoy spending money, and Hong Kong is a good place to blow the contents of a piggy bank. Older kids may go for the designer sportswear—fake and the real thing—found in the side streets of Mong Kok. Ocean Terminal has an enormous Toys'R'Us, and hundreds of shops around Nathan Road sell electronic toys and games.

Repulse Bay

What's Free

In the Top 25
10 BOTANICAL GARDENS (► 35)
21 SYMPHONY OF LIGHTS (► 46)

CHINESE UNIVERSITY OF HONG KONG ART GALLERY

This collection of Chinese art includes over 1,000 paintings and pieces of calligraphy, bronze seals from the Han Dynasty (AD25–220) and over 400 jade flower carvings.

➕ Off map to north ✉ Chinese University, Sha Tin ☎ 2609 7416
🕐 Mon–Sat 10–4.45, Sun 12.30–5.30. Closed some holidays
🚇 KCR East rail to University, then shuttle bus

CITY HALL COMPLEX

The City Hall complex has a garden where you can watch wedding parties posing for photos, plus several libraries containing rare material on microfilm, back copies of newspapers and a wealth of material on local culture and issues. Bring your passport for ID.

➕ E8 ✉ Edinburgh Place, Central ☎ 9221 2840 🕐 Libraries: Mon–Thu 10–7, Fri 10–9, Sat 10–5, Sun 10–1 🚇 Central
⛴ Star Ferry

THE HONG KONG RACING MUSEUM

This museum at the Happy Valley racecourse charts Hong Kong's love of horse-racing since the track was founded in 1884.

➕ G9 ✉ 2/F Happy Valley Stand, Happy Valley Racecourse ☎ 2966 8065 🕐 Tue–Sun 10–5. Race days 10–12.30 🚋 Happy Valley tram from Central

KOWLOON PARK

For a short wander or a rest in between shopping trips, try this little oasis. There's a statue collection, an aviary, a children's playground, some fountains and plenty of people to watch.

➕ F6 ✉ Nathan Road, Tsim Sha Tsui 🚇 Tsim Sha Tsui

LAW UK FOLK MUSEUM

A 200-year-old house furnished in Hakka style. Displays show how Hakka farmers lived, complete with furniture and farm tools.

➕ M10 ✉ 14 Kut Shing Street, Chai Wan ☎ 2896 7006 🕐 Mon–Wed, Fri, Sat 10–1, 2–6, Sun 1–6. Closed some holidays 🚇 Chai Wan

POLICE MUSEUM

Exhibitions are concerned with the history of the Hong Kong police force, triads and narcotics.

➕ F9 ✉ 27 Coombe Road, Wan Chai Gap ☎ 2849 7019
🕐 Wed–Sun 9–5, Tue 2–5 🚌 15 from Exchange Square

JUST LOOKING

There are plenty of places in Hong Kong where you can have some fun for free. It costs nothing to stand in a street market and watch the strange mix of modern bustle and ancient tradition that goes on all around you. Several small museums, including the Railway Museum in Tai Po, Flagstaff House in Hong Kong Park and the Sheung Yiu Folk Museum in Saikung, are also free.

Kowloon Park

Journeys

STAIRWAY TO HEAVEN

Special to Hong Kong is the 15-minute trip up to the Mid Levels on escalators. The series of escalators begins in Central, on Des Voeux Road beside the central market and extends through the heart of the city into suburbia. The covered escalators and walkways are on stilts above the streets, so you get a fascinating view of the life below.

In the Top 25

🄴 PEAK TRAM (► 30)
🄰🄴 STANLEY BY BUS NO. 6 OR 260 (► 50)
🄸🄴 STAR FERRY (► 40)

FERRY TO CHEUNG CHAU

An air-conditioned, first-class cabin with a bar and a sunny, open-air deck make this 40-minute ride past speeding catamarans, scruffy sampans, vast tankers and tiny golden islands a relaxing treat.

✚ D7 ✉ Outlying Islands Ferry Pier, Central 🕐 Half-hourly 6.30am–11.30pm 🚇 Central 💰 Moderate

HELICOPTER RIDES

The ultimate in sightseeing—and it ought to be at these prices (HK$1,800 per head for a 15-minute trip around the island). Other trips can be arranged as well.

✚ E8 ✉ Heliservices, 2 Ice House Street, Central ☎ 2802 0200; www.heliservices.com.hk 🕐 By arrangement 🚇 Central 💰 Expensive

Tram 8 to Kennedy Town

SHEK O BY BUS NO. 9

Shau Kei Wan was once a tiny fishing village but is now a suburb. The bus starts its journey from the Shau Kei Wan MTR station and heads out east along Shek O Road, past Tai Tam Bay with the South China Sea beyond and green hills inland. You'll find some of the best beaches in Hong Kong in and around Shek O.

✚ M8 ✉ Bus terminus, Nam On Street, Shau Kei Wan 🕐 Every 15–30 minutes 🚇 Shau Kei Wan 💰 Inexpensive

TRAM RIDE

For value, this has to be one of the best rides in the world. For HK$2.00 you can travel the length of Hong Kong Island from Kennedy Town in the west to Shau Kei Wan in the east on a double-decker tram. The top deck provides a bird's-eye view of the teeming life of Hong Kong Island.

✚ D7/M8 ✉ Central, Wan Chai ✚ Sheung Wan, Shau Kei Wan MTR 🕐 6am–1am 💰 Inexpensive

HONG KONG
where to...

EAT

Cantonese Food *64*
Other Chinese Regional Fare *65*
Pan-Asian Cuisines *66*
Japanese Food *67*
Indian Dining *68*
American & Mexican Fare *69*
European Food *70–71*

SHOP

Arts & Crafts *72*
Antiques *73*
Jewelry & Watches *74*
Computers *75*
Cameras & Electronics *76*
Men's Clothes *77*
Women's Clothes *78*
Factory Outlets *79*

BE ENTERTAINED

Theaters *80*
Concerts & Shows *81*
Sport *82*
Nightclubs *83*
Live Music *84*
Pubs/Bars *85*

STAY

Luxury Hotels *86*
Mid-Range Hotels *87*
Budget Accommodations *88*

Cantonese Food

PRICES

The restaurants in this section are in three categories shown by $; this represents Hong Kong dollars (HK$) signs. Expect to pay per person for a meal, excluding drink:

$ under HK$300
$$ HK$300–HK$600
$$$ over HK$600

DIM SUM

The most traditional of Cantonese meals, dim sum (literally "small heart") is served from early morning to late afternoon in Cantonese restaurants all over the city. The dishes–including steamed dumplings stuffed with a variety of meat and vegetable fillings–arrive in bamboo baskets piled high on a tray or trolley. As the servers circulate with the trolleys, just point at whatever takes your fancy. Popular dumplings include *har gau* (shrimps), *pai kwat* (spareribs) and *woo kok* (vegetarian). You pay according to how many dishes you consume; the average price per dish is around HK$25.

HANG FOOK LAU ($–$$)

Loud, bright, busy authentic Cantonese food at down-to-earth prices. Popular with locals for lunch. Seafood hotpot is very good and varies every day according to what is available.

✚ G8 ✉ 1/F Hay Wah Mansion, 71–85 Hennessy Road, Wan Chai ☎ 2528 2468 🕙 7am–midnight 🚇 Wan Chai

JUMBO PALACE FLOATING RESTAURANT ($$$)

Alone, this highly decorated boat is a tourist attraction in itself. A night out that begins with a free ferry ride in a small sampan across the harbor. Dim sum 7am to 5pm.

✚ Off map to south ✉ Shun Wan, Wong Chuk Hang, Aberdeen ☎ 2553 9111 🕙 Daily 1am–11pm 🚌 7, 70 from Central Bus Terminal

MAN WAH RESTAURANT ($$$)

Unlike most Chinese restaurants, the Man Wah is dimly lit, intimate and elegant, as you would expect in one of Hong Kong's best hotels. The food is excellent and worth the money.

✚ E8 ✉ Mandarin Oriental Hotel, 5 Connaught Road, Central ☎ 2522 0111 🕙 Daily noon–3, 6–11 🚇 Central

SHANG PALACE ($$$)

You can eat innovative Cantonese cuisine in the grand dining room decorated in royal gold and red. Traditional dishes such as bird's-nest soup, shark's fin and lots of seafood choices

✚ F6 ✉ Kowloon Shangri La, 64 Mody Road, Kowloon ☎ 2733 8401 🕙 Daily noon–3, 6–11 🚇 Tsim Sha Tsui

SUN YUEN HING KEE ($)

Very basic cheap-eats place with plastic tables and quiet atmosphere. Dishes of rice with tasty additions. The shop sign is in Chinese only.

✚ D8 ✉ 327–329 Queen's Road, Central ☎ 2541 2207 🕙 Daily noon–3, 6–11 🚇 Central

TAI WOO SEAFOOD RESTAURANT ($)

Serving authentic Cantonese food at reasonable prices this place is busy, well lit and very popular. Vegetarians will enjoy the beancurd dishes, while seafood lovers will enjoy king crab and deep-fried stone oysters. There is a second outlet in Tsim Sha Tsui.

✚ G8 ✉ 27 Percival Street, Causeway Bay ☎ 2893 0822 🕙 Noon–midnight 🚇 Causeway Bay

YAN TOH HEEN ($$$)

Excellent, classy, Cantonese cuisine right on the waterfront. Gorgeous place settings in green jade. Lots of awards for its cooking and ambience. Excellent business lunch, hundreds of dim sum nibbles and 24 different types of fish on the menu.

✚ F7 ✉ Intercontinental Hotel, Salisbury Road, Tsim Sha Tsui ☎ 2721 1211 🕙 Daily noon–3, 6–11.30 🚇 Tsim Sha Tsui

Other Chinese Regional Fare

AMERICAN RESTAURANT ($–$$)

A vibrant Beijing-style restaurant, with tasty dishes from the cold north of the People's Republic.

➕ F8 ✉ 20 Lockhart Road, Wan Chai ☎ 2527 7277 🕐 Daily 11.30–11.30 🚇 Wan Chai

CHINA LAN KWAI FONG ($$)

This classy restaurant serves contemporary provinical Chinese cuisine.

➕ D8 ✉ 17–22 Lan Kwai Fong, Central ☎ 2536 0968 🕐 Daily 11–11 🚇 Central

GREAT SHANGHAI RESTAURANT ($)

Shanghainese food, originating in the colder north, is not lightly stir-fried like Cantonese dishes. Cold smoked fish is a traditional starter and fish dishes, especially eels, are very popular for the main course.

➕ F6 ✉ 26 Prat Avenue, Tsim Sha Tsui ☎ 2366 8158 🕐 Daily 11–11 🚇 Tsim Sha Tsui

JUMBO FLOATING RESTAURANT ($)

This sister ship to the more expensive Jumbo Palace is good fun, especially at night, when the harbor sparkles from the roof garden.

➕ Off map to south ✉ Shum Wan, Wong Chuk Hang, Aberdeen ☎ 2553 9111 🕐 Daily 7.30am–11.30pm 🚌 7, 70 from Central Bus Terminal

NEW SILK ROAD ($$)

An unusual cuisine in Hong Kong, this place serves spicy Xinjiang Muslim food. Try mutton kebabs, or dumplings to the sound of live traditional folk songs.

➕ D8 ✉ 1/F Grand Millennium Plaza, 181 Queen's Road Central, Central ☎ 2167 8188 🕐 Daily 11–11 🚇 Central

NOODLE BOX ($)

This trendy, orange, corner eatery is famous for its stacked-high noodle soups. Happy hour noodles are available Monday to Saturday from 3 to 6pm.

➕ D8 ✉ Shop 3, 30–32 Wyndham Street, Soho, Central ☎ 2536 0571 🕐 Mon–Sat Noon–10pm 🚇 Central

PRINCE COURT RESTAURANT ($$)

The menu here does not distinguish Cantonese dishes from spicy Szechuan, so if spiciness is an issue, ask for help when you order. Special dishes include the seafood-and-bean-curd soup and the chili shrimps and noodles.

➕ F6 ✉ Shop 305, The Gateway, 25 Canton Road, Tsim Sha Tsui ☎ 2730 9131 🕐 Daily 11.30am–midnight 🚇 Tsim Sha Tsui

SICHUAN GARDEN RESTAURANT ($$)

Smoked duck, the classic of Szechuan cuisine—which is noted for its subtle use of spicing—is available here.

➕ D8 ✉ 3/F, Gloucester Tower, The Landmark, 11 Pedder Street, Central ☎ 2521 4433 🕐 Daily 11.30–3, 5.30–11.30 🚇 Central

HANDLING CHOPSTICKS

- Hold one chopstick between thumb joint and tip of third finger.
- Hold the other chopstick between tip of thumb and tips of first and second fingers.
- Keep the first chopstick rigid while moving the second one up and down to pick up the food.
- Put food from the serving dish on top of rice, hold the bowl close to your mouth and push the food in with the chopsticks. Chinese etiquette does not demand precision, and making a bit of a mess is quite acceptable.

Pan-Asian Cuisines

DRINKS

Hotel restaurants and cafés are your best bet if you're looking for a proper English tea served with fresh milk and sugar. For decent coffee look to the European–and American-style coffee booths in glitzy shopping malls. Foreign beers and spirits are readily available–try sharp-tasting *Tsingtao*, Chinese beer inspired by a German recipe. If you are not used to the local beer, *San Miguel*, you may find it gives you a hangover. Western wine is available in most restaurants.

BALI RESTAURANT ($–$$)

Good Indonesian food in fairly basic surroundings which try and fail to conjure up the atmosphere of Bali. Satay and *gado-gado* (mixed vegetable salad served with spicy peanut sauce), Indonesian fried rice and *rijstafel*, a combination of Dutch and Indonesian styles with lots of little dishes all served together on a rice base.

🚇 F5 ⊠ 10, Nanking Street, Tsim Sha Tsui ☎ 2780 2902 🕐 Daily noon–11 🚇 Jordan

THE CURRY POT ($)

Curries from across Southeast Asia and the Indian subcontinent for both vegetarians and meat-eaters.

🚇 F9 ⊠ 68–70 Lockhart Road, Wan Chai ☎ 2865 6099 🕐 Daily 6am–11pm 🚇 Wan Chai

FELIX ($$)

You'll find excellent contemporary cuisine in this modern restaurant designed by Philippe Starck. Excellent California/ Pan-Asian cuisine. Check out the chairs and, for males, the lavatories.

🚇 F6 ⊠ Peninsula Hotel, Salisbury Road, Kowloon ☎ 2366 6251 🕐 Daily 11.30–3, 6.30–11 🚇 Tsim Shu Tsui

INDOCHINE 129 ($$)

The French influence on Vietnamese food is very apparent in the menu of this restaurant, with its colonial-style setting. Good place to try out Vietnamese food for the first time.

🚇 D8 ⊠ 2/F, California Tower, 30–32 D'Aguilar Street, Central ☎ 2869 7399 🕐 Mon–Sat noon–2.30, daily 6.30–11 🚇 Central

LORD STANLEY AT THE CURRY POT ($$)

Tasty Indian food with all the spicy choices of a long Indian menu, including good vegetarian options. The restaurant overlooks the beach and is well worth the trip out for the relaxed atmosphere and excellent views.

🚇 Off map to south ⊠ Ground Floor, 92 Stanley Main Streeti ☎ 22890 0811 🕐 Daily noon–3, 6–11 🚇 Tsim Sha Tsui

MABUHAY RESTAURANT ($)

A friendly restaurant that serves Filipino and Spanish dishes at reasonable prices.

🚇 F6 ⊠ 11 Minden Avenue, Tsim Sha Tsui ☎ 2367 3762 Daily 11–11 🚇 Tsim Sha Tsui

VONG ($$$)

If your taste buds need pampering, try this much lauded restaurant in the award-winning Mandarin Oriental Hotel. Amazing views over the harbor and Thai-inspired French Vietnamese cuisine. Dishes include such delicacies as sautéed foie gras with ginger and mango, and lobster with Thai herbs.

🚇 E8 ⊠ 25/F, Mandarin Oriental, 5 Connaught Road, Central ☎ 2522 0111, ext. 4028 🕐 Daily noon–3, 6–midnight 🚇 Central

Japanese Food

AH-SO ($)
The design is Japanese, right down to the u-shaped sushi bar, and the menu offers tempura and fried prawns as well as sushi and sashimi. Service is fast, and you are not expected to sit around after eating.
E6 ✉ 122 Harbour City, Canton Road, Tsim Sha Tsui ☎ 2730 3392 🕐 Daily noon–3, 5–11 🚇 Tsim Sha Tsui

HANAGUSHI JAPANESE RESTAURANT ($$)
Yakitori (grilled meat on skewers) is the signature dish of this friendly little restaurant and is always in the set meals as well as on the menu. Try the *soba* noodles. Gets very crowded between 1 and 2pm on weekdays.
D8 ✉ 1/F Ho Lee Commercial Building, 17–22 Lan Kwai Fong, Central ☎ 2521 0868 🕐 Mon–Sat 10.30–3, 6–11 🚇 Central

MISO JAPANESE RESTAURANT ($$$)
It's not surprising this restaurant boasts excellent *miso*, which is a paste made from soy beans and rice and a staple of Japanese cuisine. This place is modernly stylish.
E8 ✉ LG/F, Jardine House, 1 Connaught Place, Central ☎ 2845 8773 🕐 Daily 11–3, 5.30–10.30 🚇 Central

SAGANO RESTAURANT ($$$)
For the Japanese chefs at this restaurant in a Japanese hotel the distinctive cuisine is *kansai* from around Kyoto. Don't miss the *teppanyaki* counter, where chefs juggle with their cooking tools.
G6 ✉ Hotel Nikko, 72 Mody Road, Tsim Sha Tsui ☎ 2739 1111 🕐 Daily noon–2.30, 6–10.30 🚇 Tsim Sha Tsui

SUN ($$)
Hong Kong's only *kamameshi* restaurant. *Kamameshi* cuisine consists of steamed dishes with rice, meat and some vegetables in a savory sauce. The chefs work in an open plan kitchen so you can watch them work while you wait.
G8 ✉ 1304 Food Forum, Times Square, Causeway Bay ☎ 2506 1838 🕐 Daily noon–3, 5–1am 🚇 Causeway Bay

TOKIO JOE ($$)
Very trendy spot in Lan Kwai Fong serving excellent sushi and sashimi as well as filled rolls and hot dishes. The same company has two more Japanese places in the area, Kyoto Joe and Joe's Yaki, which are more like *teppanyaki* bars.
D8 ✉ 16 Lan Kwai Fong, Central ☎ 2525 1889 🕐 Mon–Sat noon–2.30, 6.30–11, Sun 6.30–11 🚇 Central

YOROHACHI JAPANESE RESTAURANT ($$)
A good place to enjoy traditional tempura, *teppanyaki*, or sushi. The set meals are reasonably priced.
D8 ✉ 6 Lan Kwai Fong, Central ☎ 2524 1251 🕐 Daily 11–3, 6–11 🚇 Central

WHICH DISH?
If you are unfamiliar with Japanese food, start with one of the set meals. Raw fish comes either as sushi (wrapped in rice or seaweed) or sashimi (in slices with a horseradish sauce for dipping), or try tempura (deep-fried fish and vegetables) or *teppanyaki* (grilled meat and seafood). Many Japanese department stores have inexpensive cafés that serve most of the above.

Indian Dining

VEGETARIAN CHOICE

Vegetarians tend to look to South Indian restaurants, which don't usually serve meat but, although meaty North Indian establishments are more common in Hong Kong, vegetarians are rarely disappointed. A couple of green vegetable dishes accompanied by *raita* (yogurt) and *naan* (puffed-up wholewheat), complemented by a lentil *dal* adds to a small feast for two.

THE ASHOKA RESTAURANT ($)

Delicious curries, tandoori dishes and other fare—some vegetarian, all tasty and spicy. This place gets bonus points for cleanliness and comfort.
🔶 D8 ✉ G/F, 57 Wyndham Street, Central ☎ 2524 9623 🕐 Daily noon–2.30, 6–11.30 🚇 Central

DELHI CLUB MESS ($$)

Plush by Chungking Mansions standards (➤ 88, panel), frequented by regulars—two good reasons for a feast here.
🔶 F6 ✉ Block C, Flat 3, 3/F, Chungking Mansions, 36–44 Nathan Road, Tsim Sha Tsui ☎ 2368 1682 🕐 Daily noon–3.30, 6–11.30 🚇 Tsim Sha Tsui

GAYLORD INDIAN RESTAURANT ($$)

Starters are superb, and the breads and kebabs come fresh out of the tandoori oven. One of the best ways to try the food here is to have a lunch buffet. Cozy and pubby.
🔶 F6 ✉ 1/F, Ashley Centre, 23–5 Ashley Road, Tsim Sha Tsui ☎ 2376 1001 🕐 Daily 11.45–3, 6–11.30 🚇 Tsim Sha Tsui

JO JO MESS CLUB ($)

Probably the least expensive place for consistently good food in Wan Chai.
🔶 F9 ✉ 86 Johnston Road (entrance on Lee Tung Street), Wan Chai ☎ 2527 3776 🕐 Daily 11–3, 6–11 🚇 Wan Chai

KOH-I-NOOR ($)

A good bet for affordable meals on Hong Kong Island. The cuisine is North Indian but the spiciness is moderated; vegetarian dishes are on the menu.
🔶 D8 ✉ 1/F, 103 California Entertainment Building, 34 D'Aguilar Street, Central ☎ 2877 9706 🕐 Daily 11.30–2.30, 6–11 🚇 Central

NANAK MESS ($)

No-frills whatever—but the food is reliable, authentic and consistently tasty.
🔶 F6 ✉ Block A, Flat 4,11/F Chungking Mansions, 36–44 Nathan Road, Tsim Sha Tsui ☎ 2368 8063 🕐 Daily noon–3, 7–11 🚇 Tsim Sha Tsui

TANDOOR RESTAURANT ($$–$$$)

A classy restaurant with rosewood furniture, lunch and dinner buffets and a wide-ranging menu. Try the betelnut-based desserts.
🔶 D8 ✉ 19 Wyndham Street, Central ☎ 2845 2299 🕐 Daily noon–2.30, 6–10.45 🚇 Central

WOODLANDS INTERNATIONAL RESTAURANT ($)

In the city's only Indian vegetarian restaurant, the decor is spare but the *dosa* (rice-flour pancakes) and *thali* (set meals) are excellent and good value. No alcohol is served here.
🔶 F6 ✉ G/F, Mirror Tower, 61 Mody Road, Tsim Sha Tsui ☎ 2369 3718 🕐 Daily noon–3.30, 6.30–11 🚇 Tsim Sha Tsui

American & Mexican Fare

AL'S DINER ($$)

First-rate sirloin from the US goes into the fair-sized burgers. There's lots of 1950s chrome and neon, and a juke box churns out period songs.

D8 ✉ Room F, G/F, Winner Building, 27–37 D'Aguilar Street, Central ☎ 2869 1869 🕐 Daily 11.30am–1.30am 🚇 Central

THE BOSTONIAN ($$$)

Fresh fish, brought to your table for choosing, plus imaginative preparations and bright decor suggest California—never mind the restaurant's name. If you come for the lunch buffet, plan for a light dinner.

F6 ✉ Renaissance Hotel, 8 Peking Road, Tsim Sha Tsui ☎ 2375 1133 🕐 Daily noon –2.30, 7–11 🚇 Tsim Sha Tsui

!CARAMBA ($$)

Spicy Mexican fare with Chinese overtones is served up with plenty of tequila at this spot in chic Soho. Try the scrumptious tortilla chips. Reserve ahead for weekends.

D8 ✉ 26–30 Elgin Street, Central ☎ 2530 9963 🕐 Daily noon–midnight 🚇 Central

COYOTE ($$)

Slurp down one of the 56 varieties of margaritas, and to soak it up launch into a monstrous plate of *nachos simpaticos*.

F8 ✉ 114–120 Lockhart Road, Wan Chai ☎ 2861 2221 🕐 Daily 11.30am –midnight 🚇 Fortress Hill

DAN RYAN'S CHICAGO GRILL ($$)

Traditional choices on the menu include clam chowder, potato skins, salads and baby back ribs in barbecue sauce. The burgers are universally recognized as excellent. Leave room for brownies or carrot cake. Be sure to make a reservation—this place is popular.

F6 ✉ 200 Ocean Terminal, Harbour City, Tsim Sha Tsui ☎ 2735 6111 🕐 Mon–Fri 11am–midnight, Sat, Sun 10am–midnight. Closes 2am Fri 🚇 Tsim Sha Tsui
Also
E8 ✉ 114 Pacific Place, 88 Queensway, Central ☎ 2845 4600 🕐 Mon–Fri 11am–midnight, Sat, Sun 10am–midnight. Closes 2am Sat 🚇 Admiralty

L. A. BRASSERIE ($$)

This relaxed American-style eatery serves excellent steaks as well as an interesting east-meets-west mix of American food with a Chinese twist. Try the foie gras with Shenzen beef strips and darkened tuna. Pleasant bar to while away the hours.

F6 ✉ Regal Kowloon Hotel, 71 Mody Road, Tsim Sha Tsui ☎ 2313 8778 🕐 Daily noon–3, 6–11 🚇 Tsim Sha Tsui

RUBY TUESDAY AMERICAN GRILL ($)

Fajitas, potato skins, nachos, ribs, burgers—plus mouth-watering desserts.

E6 ✉ Shop 283, Deck 2 Ocean Terminal, Tsim Sha Tsui ☎ 2376 3122 🕐 Daily noon–10.30 🚇 Central

AFTERNOON TEA

The red pillar boxes have all been repainted green, but the British ritual of afternoon tea is still going strong. For the full works—china, chandeliers and chamber music—the Peninsula Hotel in Salisbury Road (► 86) is hard to beat, but the Grand Hyatt in Wan Chai and the Mandarin Oriental (► 86) are worthy (and equally) expensive alternatives.

European Food

EUROPE IN ASIA

Virtually every European cuisine is represented in Hong Kong and the food in the restaurants loses nothing from being transplanted to Asia. Local visitors like the more expensive hotel restaurants, while younger Hong Kong couples prefer the more informal European-style places.

HOTEL RESTAURANTS

These tend to be the most expensive dining options in Hong Kong but the service, the food and choice of wines are usually excellent. The styles–both culinary and interior design–range from the modern, such as Felix (➤ 66), to highly conventional, like Gaddi's (➤ 71).

AMIGO RESTAURANT ($$$)

Spanish setting, French fare (*filet de sole Marquis*, *crevettes au gruyère*). Set meals are less expensive and less formal at lunchtime.
⊞ G9　⊠ Amigo Mansion, 79A Wong Nei Chung Road, Happy Valley　☎ 2577 2202　⊙ Daily noon–3, 6–midnight　🚋 Tram from Central

BB'S BISTRO ($$)

New restaurant in a recently developed area of Tsim Sha Tsui, Kowloon's slightly cheaper answer to Lan Kwai Fong. Good French regional cooking, large wine list, open till very late. Sit outside and watch the late night clubbers in search of food.
⊞ F6　⊠ G/F, 13 Knutsford Terrace, Kowloon　☎ 2316 2212　⊙ Daily noon–3, 6–3am　🚇 Tsim Sha Tsui

BOCA ($$)

For a *tapas* and good wine–at a reasonable price–check out this popular Soho newcomer.
⊞ D8　⊠ 65 Peel Street, Central　☎ 2548 1717　⊙ Daily noon–11　🚇 Central

BRASSERIE ON THE EIGHTH ($$$)

Superb French fare–in small portions–with excellent service and lovely views.
⊞ E8　⊠ 8/F Conrad International Hotel, Pacific Place, Admiralty　☎ 2521 3838, ext. 8270　⊙ Daily noon–3, 6–11　🚇 Admiralty

CAMMINO ($$)

A Little Italy in the heart of Causeway Bay, this restaurant works overtime at making you feel you are somewhere else. Great Italian food from the various regions of Italy in an intimate, quiet atmosphere.
⊞ G8　⊠ The Excelsior Hotel, 281 Gloucester Road, Causeway Bay　☎ 2894 8888　⊙ Mon–Sat noon–2.30, daily 6–11　🚇 Causeway Bay

THE CHALET ($$$)

Timber, brick, stone, fondue–and the widest range of Swiss wines outside Europe.
⊞ F6　⊠ 9/F, Royal Pacific Hotel, China Hong Kong City, 33 Canton Road, Tsim Sha Tsui　☎ 2738 2388　⊙ Daily noon –2.30, 7–11　🚇 Tsim Sha Tsui

THE DUBLIN JACK ($$)

Wash down your Irish stew with a pint of Guinness. The place is packed on weekends.
⊞ D8　⊠ 37–43 Cochrane Street (next to escalators), Central　☎ 2543 0081　⊙ Daily 11am–12.30am　🚇 Central

FAT ANGELO'S ($$)

For big portions, reasonable prices and homestyle Italian cooking, this is the place. The lasagne easily feeds four people.
⊞ F6　⊠ 29–43 Ashley Road, Tsim Sha Tsui　☎ 2730 4788　⊙ Daily noon–11.30　🚇 Tsim Sha Tsui
Also at
⊞ D8　⊠ 49 A–C Elgin Street, Central　☎ 2973 6808　⊙ Daily noon–11.30　🚇 Central
and
⊞ F8　⊠ 414 Jaffe Road, Wan Chai　☎ 2574 6263　⊙ Daily noon–11.30　🚇 Wan Chai

GADDI'S ($$$)
One of Hong Kong's best restaurants is definitely a place you'll remember, especially at night if you go when the chandeliers are sparkling and the band is playing. It's popular with Asian tourists for both its fine service and French food. Reservations a must.
🚩 F6 ✉ 1/F, Peninsula Hotel, Salisbury Road, Tsim Sha Tsui ☎ 2366 6251 🕐 Daily noon–3, 6.30–11 🚇 Tsim Sha Tsui

HUGO'S ($$$)
Busy but still intimate, Hugo's is famous for the roses and cigars that are handed out for free. The Sunday brunch is a feast (reservations essential). Evenings, candlelight and serenaders make things romantic.
🚩 F6 ✉ Hyatt Regency Hotel, 67 Nathan Road, Tsim Sha Tsui ☎ 2311 1234 🕐 Mon–Sat noon–3, 7–11; Sun 11.30–3, 7–11 🚇 Tsim Sha Tsui

JIMMY'S KITCHEN ($$)
Its history stretches back to the 1920s, venerable for Hong Kong, and its menu can be relied on for its signature goulash, borscht and stroganoff. Comfortable and traditional with equally reliable service.
🚩 D8 ✉ Basement, South China Building, 1 Wyndham Street, Central ☎ 2526 5293 🕐 Daily noon–midnight 🚇 Central

THE LOBSTER BAR & GRILL ($$$)
Swanky relaxed place with live bands to serenade you.

Innovative modern European menu—try blue fin tuna with asparagus and eggplant salad or the seared chicken breast with scallops and fennel. Nice bar, too.
🚩 E8 ✉ Island Shangri-La, Pacific Place, Supreme Court Road, Central ☎ 2820 8560 🕐 Daily noon–2.30, 6.30–10 🚇 Central

THE MISTRAL ($$$)
Come here for a relaxed meal away from the Tsim Sha Tsui crowds, plus excellent pasta, pizza and other Italian dishes. Rustic Mediterranean furnishings.
🚩 G6 ✉ Basement, Grand Stanford, Harbour View, 70 Mody Road, Tsim Sha Tsui East ☎ 2721 5161 🕐 Daily noon–3, 7–11 🚇 Tsim Sha Tsui

THE PIZZERIA ($$)
North Italian pasta and pizza and a good range of regional wines.
🚩 F6 ✉ 2/F, Kowloon Hotel, 19–21 Nathan Road, Tsim Sha Tsui ☎ 2929 2888, ext. 3322 🕐 Daily 11.45–3, 6–11 🚇 Tsim Sha Tsui

SPPONS ($$$)
Everything here has a designer label, right down to the ash trays, mink seat cushions and waitresses' dresses. The classic French menu is "flexible," meaning you can order any of the main courses with any of the accompanying sauces—the waiters will advise.
🚩 F7 ✉ Intercontinental Hotel, 18, Salisbury Road, Kowloon ☎ 2313 2256 🕐 Daily 6pm–midnighnt 🚇 Tsim Sha Tsui

RESTAURANTS WITH A VIEW

The two of the best rooms with a view are Parc 27 (Park Lane Hotel, 310 Gloucester Road, Causeway Bay ☎ 2890 3355) and Vong (25/F, Mandarin Oriental, 5 Connaught Road, Central ☎ 2522 0111, ext. 4028).

Arts & Crafts

THE HKTB

Look for the HKTB logo—a red Chinese junk sailing against a white background—in shop windows. It means that the shop is registered with the Hong Kong Tourist Board and is committed to certain standards—that is, it will promptly rectify complaints and give you adequate value for money. More importantly, at these shops the HKTB will investigate and help you get redress if you choose to bring a complaint (although it does not accept liability for the behaviour of its registered members).

CHINESE EMPORIA

Chinese emporia provides perhaps the most diverse shopping in the world. You've got alley-lined markets selling knock-off goods ranging from CDs to designer handbags, huge government-owned department stores selling Made-in-China basics, and private department stores featuring merchandise from around the world. If you're looking for something distinctly "Chinese"—be it jade or cloisonette—consider pricing the items in one of the department stores before wandering Hollywood Road (► 73).

CHINA PRODUCTS

Although this is similar to the other China Products shops, this one has an added bonus— as much as 15 percent discounts to foreign-passport holders.

🚻 G8 ✉ 488–500 Hennessy Road, Causeway Bay ☎ 2577 0222 🕐 Daily 10–10 🚇 Causeway Bay

CHINESE ARTS AND CRAFTS (HK) LTD

You can find some beautiful things here— pottery, silks, embroideries, carved gemstones, clothes, furniture, carpets, tea, jewelry, statues and novelties.

🚻 F6 ✉ Star House, 3 Salisbury Road, Tsim Sha Tsui ☎ 2735 4061 🕐 Daily 10–8. Closed Chinese New Year 🚇 Tsim Sha Tsui

CHINESE ARTS AND CRAFTS (HK) LTD

Compared to other Chinese emporia, this one stocks more designer rosewood and lacquer furniture, lamps and carpets. You can find some pretty valuable pieces here.

🚻 F8 ✉ Lower Block, China Resources Building, 26 Harbour Road, Wan Chai ☎ 2827 6667 🕐 Daily 10–7.30 🚇 Wan Chai

MOUNTAIN FOLKCRAFT

Delightful handmade paintings, carvings and batik from Southeast Asia.

🚻 D8 ✉ 12 Wo On Lane, Central ☎ 2523 2817 🕐 Mon—Sat 9.30–6.30 🚇 Central

STANLEY CHINESE PRODUCTS CO LTD

This is one of several good stalls and shops around Stanley Market, all offering clothes, silks, embroideries and gift items, at competitive prices.

🚻 Off map to south ✉ 22–26 Stanley Main Street, Stanley ☎ 2813 0649 🕐 Daily 10–6.30 🚌 6 from Central Bus Terminal

TEQUILA KOLA

For well-crafted reproductions of antique bedroom sets, cabinets and dinner tables, visit this huge designer warehouse only 15 minutes from central Hong Kong. Residents don't just say they bought a table—they call it a "Tequila Kola" table. The store also has home accessories— candles, cushions, lamps mirrors and more—from across Asia, so it's a shopaholics paradise.

🚻 Off map ✉ Horizon Plaza, 2 Lee Wing Street, Ap Lei Chau Island ☎ 2877 3295 🕐 Mon–Sat 10–7, Sun noon–7 🚌 7 from Central Bus Terminal

YUE HWA CHINESE PRODUCTS EMPORIUM

A much more basic and everyday shop than the other, more centrally located Chinese emporia. Look for cheap, beautiful dinner services, embroideries, pricey and inexpensive jewelry, workaday silk items and Chinese herbal medicines.

🚻 F5 ✉ 301 Nathan Road, Kowloon ☎ 2384 0084 🕐 Daily 10–10 🚇 Jordan

Antiques

AMAZING GRACE ELEPHANT CO

Antiques, curios and gift items from around Asia. There are branches in the Excelsior Hotel shopping mall, Causeway Bay and the City Plaza at Tai Koo Shing.

✚ F6 ✉ 348–9 Ocean Centre, Harbour City, Tsim Sha Tsui ☎ 2730 5455 ⏰ Daily 9.30–7.30 🚇 Tsim Sha Tsui

ARCH ANGEL ANTIQUES

Huge antiques shop with floors of antique ceramics, professionally restored furniture, sculpture and art. They also deal in smaller pieces for the passing trade. Close by is their sister shop Arch Angel Art, which specializes in modern Vietnamese paintings.

✚ D8 ✉ 53–58 Hollywood Road, Centrali ☎ 2851 6848 ⏰ Daily 9.30–6.30 🚇 Central

THE BANYAN TREE LTD

Antiques, arts, crafts and furniture from India, the Philippines, Indonesia and South America. A branch in the Repulse Bay shopping arcade.

✚ E8 ✉ 214–218 Princes Building, Chater Road, Central ☎ 2523 5561 ⏰ Mon–Sat 10.30–7, Sun 12.30–7 🚇 Central

CAT STREET GALLERIES

This shopping complex full of antiques dealers and curio shops is located close to the Hollywood Road antiques area.

✚ D8 ✉ 38 Lok Ku Road, Sheung Wan ☎ 2541 8908 ⏰ Daily 10–6 🚇 Sheung Wan

HONEYCHURCH ANTIQUES

Browse here for antique silver, utensils, jewelry and a collection of ornaments from around the world.

✚ D8 ✉ 29 Hollywood Road, Central ☎ 2543 2433 ⏰ Mon–Sat 10–6 🚇 Central

KARIN WEBER ANTIQUES

Here you'll find a mixture of arts and crafts, modern Asian pieces and Chinese country antiques.

✚ D8 ✉ 32A Staunton Street, Soho ☎ 2544 5004 ⏰ Mon–Sat 10–6 🚇 Central

WAH TUNG CHINA CO

Several floors of wonderful pots, old and new—both individual pieces and complete Western- and Chinese-style dinner services. Check out the smaller branch is Hollywood Road, too.

✚ F9 ✉ 8 Queen's Road East, Admiralty ☎ 2520 5933 ⏰ Mon–Sat 9.30–6, Sun 11–5 🚇 Admiralty

YUE PO CHAI ANTIQUES

This established shop is worth a browse for its enormous range of antiques, knick-knacks and curios.

✚ D8 ✉ G/F, 132–6 Hollywood Road, Central ☎ 2540 4374 ⏰ Daily 9–6 🚇 Central

HOLLYWOOD ROAD

If you are a serious antiques collector or just like browsing among junk and curios, a major destination on your itinerary has to be Hollywood Road. The antiques shops start at the beginning of the road and continue for about one mile (2 km), incorporating Upper Lascar Row, which is a real flea market (open daily from around 10am until 6.30pm). Antiques that are more than 100 years old must have a certificate of authenticity. If you plan on spending a lot, you might want to check with your consulate first to find out if there will be duty charges. The importation and exportation of raw or worked ivory is governed by strict regulations. It's best to check with customs officials to find out what paperwork is required to export ivory.

Jewelry & Watches

A GEM OF A PLACE

There are more jewelry shops per head of the population in Hong Kong than in any other country. In addition to jade and pearls, many semiprecious stones are available, as well as lots of silver jewelry from around Asia. Diamonds cost about 10 percent less than elsewhere—Hong Kong is one of the world's biggest diamond markets. You should take the diamond to another vendor of your choice; this is common practice in Hong Kong. Don't just go to a shop the vendor suggests. Ask the dealers to inspect the diamond and weigh it, giving you the details about its clarity, weight and quality. Ask them to certify their opion on a certificate with their chop, or official business signature. The market at Stanley is a good place to shop for silver and beads, while any shop displaying the Hong Kong Tourist Board (HKTB) sign (➤ 72, panel) is a relatively safe bet for more expensive items.

ANITA CHAN JEWELLERY

Reasonably priced and well designed pieces, particularly interesting designs using jade and gemstones.

➕ F6 ✉ Shop LO87 & LO 89, New World Centre, 18–24 Salisbury Road, Tsim Sha Tsui ☎ 2368 9654 ⏰ Daily 9.30–6.30 🚇 Tsim Sha Tsui

CARTIER'S

One of the many classy designer jewelry shops in Hong Kong. Prices at this store are lower than in other parts of the world.

➕ F6 ✉ Peninsula Hotel, Salisbury Road, Tsim Sha Tsui ☎ 2368 8036 ⏰ Daily 10–7 🚇 Tsim Sha Tsui

CHINESE ARTS AND CRAFTS SHOPS

These shops' extensive jewelry departments sell watches and jewelry, particularly jade and gold (➤ 72).

CHOW TAI FOOK

This is just one of a good local jewelry chain that has branches in Causeway Bay, Central and around Mong Kok. Check out the jade and watch the way local people going about the serious business of buying.

➕ D8 ✉ G2 China Building, Queen's Road, Central ☎ 2523 7128 ⏰ Daily 10–7.30 🚇 Central

INTERNATIONAL PEARL CENTRE

Pearls and more pearls, plus diamonds.

➕ F6 ✉ G/F, Hankow Centre, 49 Peking Road, Tsim Sha Tsui ☎ 2366 4660 ⏰ Tue–Sun 10–7.30, Mon 10–5.30 🚇 Tsim Sha Tsui

KS SZE & SONS LTD

A good excuse to wander inside the Mandarin Oriental Hotel. Pearls are a specialty, and fair prices a commitment.

➕ E8 ✉ Shop M11, Mandarin Oriental Hotel, 5 Connaught Road, Central ☎ 2524 2803 ⏰ Mon–Sat 9.30–6 🚇 Central

LARRY JEWELRY

One of several branches of the internationally famous jeweler.

➕ E8 ✉ Shop 232, Level 2, The Mall, Pacific Place Two, 88 Queensway, Central ☎ 2868 3993 ⏰ Daily 10–7 🚇 Admiralty

OPAL MINE

This is both a shop and an exhibition about opal mining and processing. Prices are low because precious stones are not taxed when imported into Hong Kong.

➕ F6 ✉ G/F, Burlington House, 92 Nathan Road, Tsim Sha Tsui ☎ 2721 9933 ⏰ Daily 9.30–6.30 🚇 Tsim Sha Tsui

TSE SUI LUEN JEWELLERY (INTERNATIONAL LTD)

There are several branches of this store around the city, selling fairly traditional designs in jewelry, watches and more. Branches in Queen's Road, Central, Causeway Bay, Nathan Road and more.

➕ F6 ✉ Shop A&B G/F 190 Nathan Road, Tsim Sha Tsui ☎ 2926 3210 ⏰ Daily 10–10 🚇 Tsim Sha Tsui

Computers

COMPUTER MALL

A collection of specialist computer shops retailing hardware and software. Stores look more sophisticated than those in Sham Shui Po, but the selection is basically the same. ✚ G8 ✉ 11–12/F, The In Square, Windsor House, 311 Gloucester Road, Causeway Bay ⏰ Daily 11–8.30 Ⓜ Causeway Bay

GOLDEN SHOPPING CENTRE

A few stores sell computer books in English. It used to be where locals went for pirated goods since the government crack down on the trade. Still, legitimate software is sold here for less than elsewhere. ✚ E2 ✉ Golden Shopping Centre, 146–52 Fuk Wa Street, Sham Shui Po ⏰ Daily 10–10 Ⓜ Sham Shui Po (follow signs for the Golden Shopping Centre)

MONG KOK COMPUTER CENTRE

This small shopping block is crammed with tiny shops that spill out into the teeming corridors. The vendors are knowledgeable and catalogues of prices are on display. Hardware is mostly Asian-made: computers, monitors, printers and add-on boards. Warranties are usually only for Asia, but prices are competitive. ✚ F4 ✉ Mong Kok Computer Centre, 8–8a Nelson Street, Mong Kok ☎ 2781 1109 ⏰ Daily 10–10 Ⓜ Mong Kok

NEW CAPITAL COMPUTER PLAZA

The concentration of computer stores is far less dense than at the nearby Golden Shopping Centre. Discounts of 10–20 percent on software can often be negotiated. ✚ E2 ✉ 100–2 Yen Chow Street, Sham Shui Po ⏰ Daily 10–10 Ⓜ Sham Shui Po

THE NOTEBOOK SHOP

The entire second floor of Star House, known as Star Computer City, is devoted to computers and peripherals. This particular store stocks only laptop computers, including quality names such as Toshiba and IBM. Special offers are usually available. ✚ F6/F7 ✉ Unit A6–7, 2/F, Star House, 3 Salisbury Road, Tsim Sha Tsui ☎ 2736 2608 ⏰ Mon–Fri 9.30–6.30, Sat 10–7 Ⓜ Tsim Sha Tsui

WAN CHAI COMPUTER CITY

The legitimate end of the computer market. All the software here is legal with prices to match. Lots of tiny shops selling everything from PCs to laptops, personal organizers, office furniture, desk tidies. Prices here are not bargain basement and it pays to shop around even within the complex itself before you decide to buy. ✚ F8 ✉ 130 Hennessy Road, Wan Chai ⏰ Daily noon–9 Ⓜ Wan Chai

SHOPPING TIPS

Before parting with any money check whether the warranty is an international one or just for Asia. If it is the latter, the price should be lower. Always check a quote with other retailers before making a substantial purchase. When buying software, make sure you know the specs of your hardward and check the minimum memory and speed requirements on the box before you buy. Prices in Hong Kong are comparable to those in the US; Europeans will find some good bargains.

Cameras & Electronics

SHOPPING TIPS

Before you leave home, check prices on the kinds of items you may be tempted to buy. Despite Hong Kong's longstanding reputation as a source of low prices on camera and electronics, prices can be higher than in the US. Avoid shops that do not display prices. Get quotes from various dealers and try haggling a little. Finally, if you do make a purchase, use a credit card, and watch carefully as your acquisition is put back into its box and then into a bag—many dealers won't take stuff back after you've left the store.

Look for the HKTB logo displayed in stores; they also supply free special interest pamphlets including their *Official Shopping Guide* and shopping guides to buying electronics and jewelry.

BROADWAY PHOTO SUPPLY

This is the biggest branch of a Hong Kong-wide electrical chain that sells everything from washing machines to electric razors. Most major brands are available at marked down prices, which are more or less fixed, although you might get a free gift thrown in. You can get a good idea here of a sensible local price, and then move on to serious haggling in some smaller, pushier place if that's what you really want to do.

✚ F4 ✉ G/F and 1/F, 731 Nathan Road, Mong Kok ☎ 2394 3827 🕐 Mon–Sat 10.30–9.30; Sun 11.30–9.30 🚇 Mong Kok

FORTRESS

A major rival of Broadway offering a similar range of cameras, sound equipment, camcorders, electronics, electronic games and so on, all at fixed prices. There are dozens of branches throughout the city, but this one is good for reconnaissance before setting off on a major haggling trip. Buy here and enjoy a hassle-free holiday, but if you like the cut and thrust of bargaining, then this should at least be your first stop.

✚ F6 ✉ Shop 281, Ocean Terminal, Harbour City, Canton Road, Tsim Sha Tsui ☎ 2735 8628 🕐 Mon–Fri 10.30–7.30, Sat, Sun and holidays 10–8 🚇 Tsim Sha Tsui

PHOTO SCIENTIFIC

Has a great reputation for good, if not cheap, prices for camera equipment and is especially liked by professional users. No bargaining here—pay up. This street has several other camera equipment shops, so if you want to shop around you don't have far to go.

✚ D8 ✉ G/F, 6 Stanley Street, Central ☎ 2525 0550 🕐 Mon–Sat 9–7 🚇 Central

SHA TIN

This area out towards the racecourse is full of small electronics shops, as well as branches of the major electrical outlets. Prices are likely to be marked and fixed. You might also try the two department stores, Seiyu and Yaohan. Don't go on Sunday or you will find yourself among what seems like the entire population of the New Territories.

✚ Off map to north 🚇 Sha Tin

WILLIAM'S PHOTO SUPPLY

A major competitor of Photo Scientific, this store also deals with cognoscenti. Again, you will find no great bargains, but if you are searching for that special something it might just be here. Besides cameras there is the usual range of binoculars and the like.

✚ D8 ✉ 138B Prince's Building, 10 Chater Road, Central ☎ 2522 8437 🕐 Mon–Sat 10–6.30 🚇 Central

Men's Clothes

ASCOT CHANG
A Hong Kong shirt-making institution.
✚ F6 ✉ Peninsula Hotel, Tsim Sha Tsui ☎ 2367 8319; www.ascotchang.com
🕐 Mon–Sat 9–7, Sun 9–5
🚇 Tsim Sha Tsui

CAUSEWAY BAY
This is a major shopping area, less touristy than Central or Tsim Sha Tsui. Here is the enormous Times Square mall (▶ 59) and four Japanese department stores—Matsuzakaya, Mitsukoshi, Daimaru and Sogo—all with several designer outlets, Marks & Spencer is here, as are all the local chain stores and Lane Crawford, a classy Southeast Asian department store.
✚ G8 🚇 Causeway Bay

THE LANDMARK
Men's stores here include Gentlemen Givenchy, Hugo, Ballantyne Boutique, Basile, Etienne Aigner, Jaeger, Benetton, Lanvin, Missoni and the Swank Shop. Prices are worth comparing with those for the same names in the US. However, in the nearby Pedder Building, factory outlets sell the same labels at even lower prices (▶ 58, 79).

OCEAN CENTRE
This and the connecting malls have branches of Carpe Diem, Ermenegildo Zegna, Francescati, Gentlemen Givenchy, Hugo, Swank Shop, as well as an excellent Marks & Spencer and local chain stores such as Giordano, G2000 and U2.
✚ F6 ✉ Harbour City, 5 Canton Road, Tsim Sha Tsui
🕐 Daily 10–8 🚇 Tsim Sha Tsui

PACIFIC PLACE
A collection of designer outlets and local chain stores. This mall has an Alfred Dunhill, Ermenegildo Zegna, Hugo, Swank Shop, plus a Marks & Spencer, Lane Crawford and several local retailers selling casual separates at basic prices (▶ 59).

SAM'S
Another Hong Kong institution, numbering the Duke of Kent among its clientele.
✚ F6 ✉ Burlington Arcade K, 92–4 Nathan Road, Tsim Sha Tsui ☎ 2367 9423; www.samtailor.com 🕐 Mon–Sat 10.30–7.30, Sun 10–12
🚇 Tsim Sha Tsui

W. W. CHAN & SONS
Suits made by this very classy tailor have a lifespan of about 20 years and will be altered free of charge during that time. Once they have taken your measurements, you can order another suit from home.
✚ F6 ✉ A2, 2/F, Burlington House, 94 Nathan Road, Tsim Sha Tsui ☎ 2366 9738
🕐 Mon–Sat 9–6
🚇 Tsim Sha Tsui

MADE TO MEASURE

Perhaps the most distinctive aspect of men's clothes in Hong Kong is the number and quality of tailors and the excellent prices of their products compared to almost everywhere. If you intend to have a suit made in Hong Kong, you should make finding a tailor that you like a priority, since the more time and fittings he can have the better the suit will be: a good tailor can make a suit in as little as 24 hours, but a few days will yield a better, less expensive suit. Some tailors offer a mail order service. See Ascot Chang and W. W. Chan, left, and Irene Fashions (▶ 78).
If you have a suit that fits perfectly, you might want to ask the tailor to duplicate it.

Women's Clothes

SHOP 'TIL YOU DROP

The really swank place to go for women's clothes is the Landmark, where every big European name is represented, including Versace, Issey Miyake, Armani, Hermes, Loewe and Nina Ricci. Other shopping complexes (▶ 58–59) all have an interesting range of clothes and labels. Note that shops aimed more at the local market tend to stock smaller sizes and popular, frillier styles with fur lining or sequins. Most local shoe shops don't stock sizes larger than 6 or 7.

CHINESE ARTS AND CRAFTS (HK) LTD, TSIM SHA TSUI

This shop sells the most glorious silk lingerie, as well as embroidered *cheong sams* (a straight dress with a side slit), jackets, crocheted silk sweaters and shawls and kimonos. Quality varies and cannot always be relied upon (▶ 72).

IRENE FASHIONS

This respected women's tailor takes several days and at least two fittings to make a suit. Have something you like copied, or choose the material and pattern at the shop.

➕ D8 ✉ Room 1102–3, 11/F Tung Chai Building, 86–90 Wellington Street, Central ☎ 2850 5635 🕔 Mon–Sat 9–6 🚇 Central

PACIFIC PLACE

Look for designer wear in Lane Crawford and Seibu department stores, T-shirts in local chain stores such as U2 and Giordano. Cotton Collection sells attractive cotton dresses, and Jessica has some elegant but inexpensive outfits (▶ 59).

STANLEY MARKET

Interesting stalls sell all sorts of things, including discounted Monsoon clothes, sportswear, Indian prints, silk garments, amusing T-shirts and designer jeans.

➕ Off map to south ✉ Stanley 🚌 Bus 6 or 260 from Central Bus Terminal

TIMES SQUARE

When you have blazed through this mall there is more shopping near by—in the streets around Causeway Bay, including Marks & Spencer, the electronics mega chain store, Fortress and the Excelsior Hotel shopping arcade (▶ 59).

TOKYU

This reasonably priced department store has a whole arcade of local designer boutiques, as well as all the big names. Clothes range from young, inexpensive casuals to classy, costly evening gowns. There is also some good sportswear.

➕ F7 ✉ New World Shopping Centre, Salisbury Road, Tsim Sha Tsui ☎ 2722 0102 🕔 Daily 10–9 🚇 Tsim Sha Tsui

VINCENT SUM DESIGNS

A handicraft shop that stocks lots of interesting and pretty batik cloth as well as clothes made from ethnic prints.

➕ D8 ✉ 15 Lyndhurst Terrace, Central ☎ 2542 2610 🕔 Daily 10–6 🚇 Central

VOGUE ALLEY

A whole shopping complex dedicated to boutiques for local-designers. Predominantly young clothes.

➕ G8 ✉ Paterson and Kingston streets, Causeway Bay 🚇 Causeway Bay

Factory Outlets

AH CHOW FACTORY

Chinese pottery and tableware, often very good quality or seconds. Nearby are clothing factory outlets along Castle Peak Road, well worth a stroll for what you might find.

✚ C1 ✉ Block B, 7F, 1 and 2 Hong Kong Industrial Centre, Castle Peak Road, Lai Chi Kok ☎ 2745 1511 🕒 Daily 10–6. Phone for appointment 🚇 Lai Chi Kok

DIANE FREIS FACTORY OUTLET

This well-known local designer's factory sells dresses and evening gowns at about 30 percent off.

✚ L5 ✉ World Interest Building, 8 Tsun Yip Lane, Kwun Tong ☎ 2362 1760 🕒 Mon–Fri 9.30–5.30, Sat 9.30–12.30 🚇 Kwun Tong

FA YUEN STREET

Better known for its street market (► 56), this is also home to a series of factory outlet shops. Labels are usually cut out, but you can find Marks & Spencer, Laura Ashley, Next, Saks, Victoria's Secret and many other European and US clothes at reductions of around 50 percent (or more).

✚ F3 ✉ Fa Yuen Street, Mong Kok 🕒 Daily 10–6 🚇 Prince Edward

HUNG HOM

The Kaiser estates are two blocks of mainly clothing factories, many with shops inside. The factories make clothes for department stores all over the world and their shops sell seconds or overruns with the labels cut out. There are also jewelry outlets here. However, this is not a leisurely place to shop. Be prepared to dig through piles of clothes and trek through the blocks of Hung Hom. Wear sensible shoes.

✚ G5–H5 🚇 Tsim Sha Tsui then taxi

LAN KWAI FONG

Several boutiques and shops sell clothes at reduced prices in this area, notably CCC, Gat and Whispers; all stock some well-known names at good prices.

✚ D8 ✉ Central 🚇 Central

PEDDER BUILDING

Five floors of tiny shops, all with something worth poking around for. Not all are factory outlets, and some sell both regular designer stuff and discounted items, so browse carefully.

✚ D8 ✉ 12 Pedder Street, Central 🚇 Central

TIMOTHY FASHION

Both men's and women's clothes. Good buys vary from season to season—look for woollen sweaters in fall, silk shirts and dresses in summer.

✚ H5 ✉ Kaiser Estate, Phase 1, 41 Man Yue Street, Hung Hom ☎ 2362 2389 🕒 Mon–Sat 9.30–6.30 🚇 Tsim Sha Tsui then taxi

BARGAIN BAZAARS

There are two major areas to look for bargains—in the Pedder Building on Hong Kong Island for the real big names, and around the factories themselves in Hung Hom in Kowloon. Granville Road in Tsim Sha Tsui is another place full of small shops selling anything from rubbish to amazing bargains, but you have to be dedicated to find the really good things. What you are likely to find is samples, seconds and overruns, often with the labels cut out. Women's clothes come mainly in small sizes, but sometimes larger bodies are catered for.

Theaters

RESERVATIONS

By quoting your passport number, you can reserve tickets for most venues by phone (or pay for them by credit card) at computerized central URBTIX offices (☎ 2734 9009) between 10am and 8pm. Check tourist literature (➤ 91) to see what's on. Ticket prices vary from about HK$600 for a good seat at a top event to HK$60 for a lesser event. City Hall and the Arts Centre, where there are URBTIX outlets, are good places to peruse promotional posters.

All the venues on this page have performances in English. It is clearly advertised if they are in Cantonese only.

FRINGE CLUB

The main venue for non-mainstream performance art, as well as interesting drama workshops. During the Arts Festival (➤ 81) alternative offerings are usually here. Often the themes are local and feature amateur actors—check press.

✚ D8 ✉ 2 Lower Albert Road, Central ☎ 2521 7251 🚇 Central

GOETHE INSTITUTE

The German Cultural Institute regularly organizes films, exhibitions and events to do with German culture and language in the Hong Kong Arts Centre.

✚ F8 ✉ 14/F, Hong Kong Arts Centre, 2 Harbour Road, Wan Chai ☎ 2802 0088 🚇 Wan Chai

HONG KONG ACADEMY FOR PERFORMING ARTS

This arts school next to the Arts Centre. has different-sized theaters, plus an outdoor venue. Concentration is on classical dance, drama and music.

✚ F8 ✉ 1 Gloucester Road, Wan Chai ☎ 2584 8500; www.hkapa.edu 🚇 Wan Chai

HONG KONG ARTS CENTRE

Drama and music of diverse kinds take place here. Ticket prices tend to be lower than at the Cultural Centre and City Hall.

✚ F8 ✉ 2 Harbour Road, Wan Chai ☎ 2582 0200; www.hkac.org.hk 🚇 Wan Chai

HONG KONG CITY HALL

The stage, auditorium and recital hall here host a wide variety of local and visiting artists.

✚ E8 ✉ 7 Edinburgh Place, Central ☎ 2921 2840; www.lcd.gov.hk/ce/cultural service/cityhall 🚇 Central

HONG KONG COLISEUM

This is the largest venue in Hong Kong for rock concerts and sporting events, with some 12,000 seats.

✚ G6 ✉ 9 Cheong Wan Road, Hung Hom, Kowloon ☎ 2355 7234 🚇 Tsim Sha Tsui then taxi

HONG KONG CULTURAL CENTRE

The premier location for orchestral music, ballet and theater. There's usually an international event of one genre or another on the schedule.

✚ F7 ✉ 10 Salisbury Road, Tsim Sha Tsui ☎ 2734 9009 🚇 Tsim Sha Tsui

SHA TIN TOWN HALL

The large gray Town Hall at this New Territories community has good acoustics, and frequently hosts international artists, especially orchestras. To get there, exit the Sha Tin MTR station, walk straight through the huge shopping complex and out the other side; the Town Hall is next to the library.

✉ 1 Yeun Wo Road, New Town Plaza, Sha Tin ☎ 2694 2511 🚇 Sha Tin

Concerts & Shows

ARTS FESTIVAL

This highly recommended event lasts four weeks and features international orchestras, dance and drama, from opera and classical music to jazz, and from folk dance to ballet. Successful productions from Europe, Asia and the US also visit. Tickets are often available at the last minute.
🕑 Mid-Feb to mid-Mar

CHINESE CULTURAL SHOWS

The best way to catch a performance of a traditional dance or one of the other classical Chinese art forms is to check with Hong Kong Tourist Board (HKTB (▶ 91). Performances range from acrobatics, puppetry and magic shows to martial arts and folk dancing. Venues all over the territory.

CHINESE OPERA AT TEMPLE STREET NIGHT MARKET

Largely amateur performances—lively and enthusiastic—take place irregularly, most commonly around the time of Chinese festivals. Songs are in Cantonese. For details contact the HKTB (▶ 91).
➕ F5–6 ✉ Temple Street, Mong Kok 🚇 Mong Kok

FESTIVAL OF ASIAN ARTS

This biennial event, held in even-numbered years, provides an opportunity to see music, dance and drama from all over Asia—it's a peerless opportunity to catch performances by artists that are rarely put on elsewhere.
🕑 Oct–Nov

HONG KONG CHINESE ORCHESTRA

Chinese orchestral music is tonally different from Western music, and a performance that uses the full range of traditional Chinese instruments is well worth finding. For schedules contact the HKTB (▶ 91).

HONG KONG DANCE COMPANY

The regular performances of this troupe, which has been choreographing new and traditional Chinese dances for over 25 years now, are a fascinating spectacle. Details from the HKTB (▶ 91).
☎ 2583 2642

HONG KONG PHILHARMONIC ORCHESTRA

A large, international orchestra with regular performances, often on weekends, in the Cultural Centre and City Hall. Ticket prices increase when a prestigious conductor arrives.

INTERNATIONAL FILM FESTIVAL

New films from around the world. Evening tickets sell quickly but tickets for other screenings are usually available at short notice.
🕑 Early Apr

CHINESE OPERA

Dating back to the 12th century, this is a highly stylized but very energetic art form. The basic story lines follow the Chinese myths. Characters wear startling make-up and gorgeous clothes. Though the Cantonese songs and accompaniment are loud and discordant to Western ears, the acrobatics and swordfights can be stunning. If you find an opera to watch, you will know it is a genuine cultural experience, not geared to tourists. Watch it as a spectacle rather than a story. The audience chats, wanders about and sometimes joins in.

Sport

AWAY FROM IT ALL

If you stay in Hong Kong long enough—and this may be just days, or even hours—the need to escape the crowds and enjoy some recreation becomes irresistible. Take a jog along Bowen Road (➤ 22) at any time of the day, an early morning or late evening jog along the Waterfront Promenade in Tsim Sha Tsui or a run up Victoria Peak (➤ 30). The Hash House Harriers (☎ 2376 2299) also organize regular runs.

SWIMMING

There are sandy beaches with safe swimming that are netted-off (to ward off shark attacks—although sometimes beaches close for shark alerts), but they are very crowded on weekends, and hence, often polluted. Lifeguards are on duty from April to September.

CHEUNG SHA

✉ Lantau Island ⛴ Outlying Islands Pier, Central, then bus from Silvermine Bay

DEEP WATER BAY

✉ South side of Hong Kong Island 🚌 7 from Central Bus Terminal to Aberdeen, then 73

REPULSE BAY

✉ South side of Hong Kong Island 🚌 6, 61 from Central

SHEK O

✉ Southeast side of Hong Kong Island 🚌 9 from Shau Kei Wan

SILVERSTRAND

✉ Sai Kung Peninsula, New Territories 🚇 Choi Hung then bus 92 or taxi

STANLEY BEACH

✉ South side of Hong Kong Island 🚌 6, 260 from Central Bus Terminal

GOLF

CLEARWATER BAY GOLF AND COUNTRY CLUB

A par-70, 18-hole, pro championship course. The golf course has stunning views.

✉ Lot #227 in DD 241, Po Toi O, Sai Kung, New Territories

☎ 2719 1595 🕐 Mon–Fri 7.30–6 🚇 Choi Hung MTR, then bus 92 💵 Green fees HK$1,400

DISCOVERY BAY GOLF CLUB

You need a whole day to enjoy a game at this 18-hole layout on outlying Lantau Island (➤ 20, 26).

✉ Valley Road, Discovery Bay, Lantau Island ☎ 2987 7273 🕐 Mon–Fri 8.30–3.15 ⛴ Outlying Islands Pier, Central 💵 Green fees HK$550–900

HONG KONG GOLF CLUB

The famous golf club with a 36-hole course has practice putting greens. Three additional (more expensive) 18-hole courses are at Fanling, New Territories (☎ 2670 1211), and are also open to visitors.

✉ 19 Island Road, Deep Water Bay, Hong Kong Island ☎ 2812 7070 🕐 May–Aug Mon–Fri 9.30–2.30; Sep–Apr Mon–Fri 9.30–1.30. Closed first Tue of every month 🚌 Minibus 6 from Central Bus Terminal 💵 Green fees HK$600

JOCKEY CLUB KAU SAI CHAU PUBLIC GOLF COURSE

There are two, 18-hole courses designed by Gary Player and a driving range at this public golf course.

✉ Kau Sai Chu, Sai Kung, New Territories ☎ 2791 3388 🕐 Daily 7am–8pm 🚇 Choi Hung MTR, then bus 92 or Green Minibus No. 1A to Sai Kung Bus Terminal. Proceed to the waterfront where you board the golf course's ferry for Kai Sai Cha 💵 Green fees HK$350–900

Nightclubs

CLUB 97

Sultry Moroccan-style café, bar and club, open 24 hours on weekends. ✚ D8 ✉ UG/F Cosmos Building, 9–11 Lan Kwai Fong, Central ☎ 2186 1897 🕐 Mon–Thu 6am–2am, Sat, Sun 8am–4am 🚇 Central

CLUB ING

Draws hip young Hong Kong girls; this place tries to bill itself as *très* chic, but many say it's missing the mark. Still it's packed every weekend. ✚ F8 ✉ 4/F, New World Harbour View Hotel, 1 Harbour Road, Wan Chai ☎ 2824 0523 🕐 Mon–Sat 5pm–4am 🚇 Wan Chai

DROP

This is the seriously cool place to be and comes highly recommended by locals and visitors alike. It's very small and so has a members only restriction at weekends, which is loosely enforced. Early evening it's a cocktail lounge serving fresh fruit cocktails and later resident DJs and Guests take over in this relaxed little place. ✚ D8 ✉ On Lok Mansion, 39–43 Hollywood Road, Central ☎ 2543 8856 🕐 Tue 7pm–2am, Wed 7pm–4 am, Thu 7pm–5am, Fri 10pm–5am, Sat, Sun 8pm–4am 🚇 Central

INSOMNIA

This place has been around long enough to have collected a loyal band of clientele. Two bars and live music after 10.30. Happy hours from 5–9. The place fills up in the early hours and especially so on weekends. All day (and night) menu of simple dishes. ✚ D8 ✉ Ho Lee Commercial Building, 34–44 D'Aguilar Street, Central ☎ 2525 0957 🕐 Mon–Sat 9am–6am, Sun 2pm–5am 🚇 Central

JOE BANANAS

Very trendy American-style bar, disco and restaurant. Long hours at weekends; men must wear a shirt with collar. Happy hours 11am–9pm. ✚ F8 ✉ 23 Luard Road, Wan Chai ☎ 2529 1811 🕐 Daily Mon–Thu 11am–5am, Fri–Sat 11am–6am, Sun and holidays noon–4am 🚇 Wan Chai

NEPTUNE

Live music and DJs entertain multiracial dancers. The cover charge varies with the season and the day, but in general this place offers the most dancing for the least money. ✚ F8 ✉ 98–108 Jaffe Road, Wan Chai ☎ 2865 2238 🕐 Daily 9pm–5.30am 🚇 Wan Chai

PEBBLES

Lots of rocks are the theme of the decor of this place but not so rocky to visit. Excellent DJs and a great atmosphere in the cool blue-lit venue. Great house cocktails, too. ✚ D8 ✉ 975 Wyndham Street, Central ☎ 2552 2628 🕐 Mon–Thu 5pm–2am, Fri–Sun 5pm–4am 🚇 Central

COVER CHARGES

Always telephone discos before you go to confirm the hours and cover charge. Many places have reduced rates during the week and/or include one or two drinks in the price. Expect to pay HK$100+ on Friday and Saturday.

Live Music

NIGHTLIFE ON THE ISLAND

Lan Kwai Fong, in Central, is where the see-and-be-seen crowd spends their money on over-priced drinks. Wan Chai, once seedy, is now one of the hippest nightlife areas in town. Soho (south of Hollywood Road) is a popular dining and drinking area for expats. Stanley is unique—more relaxed and meditative than other areas.

CARNEGIE'S

An interesting nightspot where the music shifts genre regularly but is often from local bands. It's loud and there's usually a crush on the dance floor. Cover charge only for men on weekends.

✚ F8 ✉ 53 Lockhart Road, Wan Chai ☎ 2866 6289 ⏰ Thu 7pm–10pm, Sat 7pm–midnight; Sun 7pm–11pm 🚇 Wan Chai

DELANEY'S

The design re-creates a Victorian Irish general store-cum-pub, and there's live traditional music and Irish food—even Guinness. In the branch in Luard Road, there is a Sunday evening jam session.

✚ F6 ✉ G/F, Multifield Plaza, 3–7a Prat Avenue, Tsim Sha Tsui ☎ 2301 3980 ⏰ Mon–Thu noon–3am, Fri–Sat noon–5am, Sun noon–2am 🚇 Tsim Sha Tsui
Also at
✚ F8 ✉ 2/F, 18 Luard Road, Wan Chai ☎ 2804 2880 ⏰ Mon–Thu noon–3am, Fri–Sat noon–5am, Sun noon–2am 🚇 Wan Chai

HARDY'S FOLK CLUB

Not as folksy as its name suggests but still a viable alternative to the heavy metal, rock and jazz venues. Come just for a drink, or have a meal.

✚ D8 ✉ 35 D'Aguilar Street, Central ☎ 2522 4448 ⏰ Daily 5.30pm–2am 🚇 Central

THE JAZZ CLUB

Too many places in Hong Kong are squashed into anonymous buildings, but the cramped confines here are just what is required. The Jazz Club, one of the few places you can count on for quality jazz, regularly features musicians from all over the world; drinks are reasonably priced, and cover charges, high for big names, are dropped for local acts. Seats can be reserved but must be claimed before 9pm at weekends. The alternative atmosphere and lively audience make for a great night out.

✚ D8 ✉ 2/F, California Building, 34–6 D'Aguilar Street, Central ☎ 2845 8477 ⏰ Daily 9.30pm–2am 🚇 Central

NED KELLY'S LAST STAND

The best place in Hong Kong for traditional and Dixieland jazz, belted out by a resident band. Expect a convivial atmosphere, pub food and no cover charge.

✚ F6 ✉ 11a Ashley Road, Tsim Sha Tsui ☎ 2376 0562 ⏰ Daily 9pm–2am 🚇 Tsim Sha Tsui

THE WANCH

Sociable and deservedly popular place, this former folk club, now has rock instead—usually very good music indeed. Reasonably priced as well, so things can get crowded; arrive early. No cover charge.

✚ F8 ✉ 54 Jaffe Road, Wan Chai ☎ 2861 1621 ⏰ Daily 9pm–2am 🚇 Wan Chai

Pubs/Bars

DICKENS BAR
A Dickensian place that's one of Hong Kong's best bars. Bands change constantly—Irish, West, Indian, Indonesian and Filipino—and there's jazz Sunday afternoons.
🕀 G8 ✉ LG/F, Excelsior Hotel, 281 Gloucester Road, Causeway Bay ☎ 2894 8888 🕐 Sun–Wed 11am–1am, Thu–Sat 11am–2am 🚇 Causeway Bay

DRAGON-I
The coolest bar in Hong Kong where all the really neat people go. Bar, restaurant and a terrace overlooking Wyndham Street. Lots of dancing too. Happy hours 6pm–9pm.
🕀 G8 ✉ UG/F The Centrium, 60 Wyndham Street, Central ☎ 3110 1222 🕐 Mon–Sat noon–midnight 🚇 Central

THE DUBLIN JACK
Packed with regulars on weekends, this friendly place fills to overflowing towards the end of the week, as it's *the* established pub for Central office workers.
🕀 D8 ✉ 37–43 Cochrane Street (next to escalator), Central ☎ 2543 0081 🕐 Daily 11am–12.30am 🚇 Central

FELIX
At the top of the Peninsula Hotel and attached to the famous Felix restaurant. Long marble cocktail bar serves stylish fruit cocktails.
🕀 F6 ✉ 28/F Peninsula Hotel, Salisbury Road, Tsim Sha Tsui ☎ 2315 3188 🕐 Daily 6am–2am 🚇 Tsim Sha Tsui

LA DOLCE VITA
Popular with office workers in the early evening, but a great place for people watching by night.
🕀 D8 ✉ Cosmos Building, 9–11 Lan Kwai Fong ☎ 2186 1888 🕐 Mon–Thu 11.30am–2am, Fri 12.30–3am, Sat 12.30–3am, Sun 4pm–1am 🚇 Central

MAD DOGS
This cosmopolitan bar attracts tourists and locals alike. Moved from its original location in Kowloon, it has DJs playing six nights a week and a hearty English menu of sausages and mashed potato, fish and chips. Happy hours 11am–10pm.
🕀 D8 ✉ Century Square, 1 D'Anguilar Street, Lan Kwai Fong ☎ 2810 1000 🕐 Mon–Thu 10am–2am, Fri, Sat 10am–3am 🚇 Tsim Sha Tsui

OSCAR'S
Very trendy, fan-cooled bar opening on to the street. The food is good in the separate restaurant, but the main activity is amiable drinking and chatting.
🕀 D8 ✉ G/F and basement, 2 Lan Kwai Fong, Central ☎ 2804 6561 🕐 Mon–Sat 11am–2pm, Sun 11am–midnight 🚇 Central

STAUNTON'S WINE BAR & CAFÉ
Packed to the gills most nights, this bar by the Soho escalators remains one of the most popular in town.
🕀 D8 ✉ 16A Staunton Street ☎ 2869 7652 🕐 Daily 9am–midnight 🚇 Central

NIGHTLIFE IN KOWLOON
Because of its budget accommodation, Kowloon has lots of inexpensive, casual bars, many with an Australian flavor, such as the Kangaroo, overlooking Kowloon Park, and Ned Kelly's. In addition, there are the many hostess bars, where a drink and a girl to talk to come in a package. Some of these, including Bottoms Up in Hankow Road, are almost a national institution.

85

Luxury Hotels

HOTEL PRICES

Expect to pay the following prices per night for a double room:

Luxury over HK$1,500
Mid-range HK$900–HK$1,500
Budget under HK$900

HONG KONG ISLAND

THE EXCELSIOR

Pleasant and casual with nice rooms and an enormous range of facilities, right down to the two covered tennis courts on the roof. Convenient to shopping and nightlife.

➕ G8 ✉ 281 Gloucester Road, Causeway Bay ☎ 2894 8888; www.mandarin oriental.com/excelsior 🚇 Causeway Bay

ISLAND SHANGRI-LA

Towering above Central with amazing views over the city this luxurious hotel has spacious, well-designed rooms, some great places to eat and drink, and the world's longest Chinese painting. Good fitness suite and pool. Library for guests.

➕ E8 ✉ Pacific Place, Supreme Court Road, Central ☎ 2877 3838; www. shangri-la.com 🚇 Central

MANDARIN ORIENTAL

The very central Mandarin Oriental has a long tradition of impeccable service. Well-appointed rooms, with superb attention to detail. Helpful staff, classy shops, great pool, excellent restaurants.

➕ E8 ✉ 5 Connaught Road, Central ☎ 2522 0111; www.mandarinoriental.com 🚇 Central

RITZ CARLTON

A beautiful and elegant boutique hotel with a special sense of good service, the Ritz Carlton offers guests excellent details—limousine service, fitness and swimming facilities, a good Chinese restaurant and a 24-hour maid service. Lovely classical rooms, nice views.

➕ D7 ✉ 3 Connaught Road, Central ☎ 2877 6666; www.ritz-carlton-hk.com 🚇 Central

KOWLOON

INTERCONTINENTAL HONG KONG

Simple, elegant place, with lots of good *feng shui*. Some of the best views in Kowloon straight across the harbor to the island. Amazing swimming pool. Award-winning Cantonese restaurant.

➕ F6 ✉ 18 Salisbury Road, Tsim Sha Tsui ☎ 2721 2111; www.hongkong-ic.inter continental.com 🚇 Tsim Sha Tsui

KOWLOON SHANGRI-LA

Centrally placed hotel right in the epicenter of Tsim Sha Tsui, but in atmosphere a million miles from the noise and bustle.

➕ G8 ✉ 64 Mody Road, Tsim Sha Tsui ☎ 2721 2111; www.shangri-la.com 🚇 Tsim Sha Tsui

THE PENINSULA

A landmark, cultural icon and tourist attraction in its own right, this is the last word in style. Very popular afternoon tea.

➕ F6 ✉ Salisbury Road, Tsim Sha Tsui ☎ 2366 6251; fax 2722 4170; www.hongkong. peninsula.com 🚇 Tsim Sha Tsui

Mid-Range Hotels

HONG KONG ISLAND

NEWTON

A little way out but you get a good, efficiently run hotel with a Shanghainese restaurant, close to the MRT with a shuttle service to the airport, outdoor pool and internet. Small but well appointed rooms
➕ Off map to north ✉ 218 Electric Road, North Point ☎ 2807 2333; www.newton hk.com 🚇 Fortress Hill

THE WESLEY

Close to train, tram and bus routes, with a café and decent international restaurant.
➕ F8 ✉ 22 Hennessy Road, Wan Chai ☎ 2866 6688; fax 2866 6633 🚇 Wan Chai

KOWLOON

EATON

Large with a range of room rates, as well as restaurants and a bar (but no pool or sports amenities). Catch any bus stopping outside the door to get to Tsim Sha Tsui.
➕ F5 ✉ 380 Nathan Road, Yau Ma Tei ☎ 2782 1818; fax 2782 5563 🚇 Jordan

GUANGDONG

A modest, well run place in the middle of Tsim Sha Tsui. with all the necessary requirements: two good restaurants, a fitness suite, all close to the MRT.
➕ F6 ✉ 18 Prat Avenue, Tsim Sha Tsui ☎ 3410 8888; www.gdhk.gdhotels.net 🚇 Tsim Sha Tsui

IMPERIAL

No restaurants or nightlife here, but plenty at this end of Nathan Road.
➕ F6 ✉ 30–4 Nathan Road, Tsim Sha Tsui ☎ 2366 2201; www.imperialhotel.com.hk 🚇 Tsim Sha Tsui

NATHAN

Big rooms in this relatively small and quiet place close to Jordan MRT. Well run, with everything you need to get by, including a babysitting service.
➕ F5 ✉ 378 Nathan Road, Tsim Sha Tsui ☎ 2388 5141; www.nathanhotel.com 🚇 Jordan

THE SALISBURY

This 366-room YMCA has a good location that's convenient to the shops and theStar Ferry, plus an inexpensive self-service restaurant and free use of a swimming pool.
➕ F6 ✉ 41 Salisbury Road, Tsim Sha Tsui ☎ 2369 2211; fax 2739 9315 🚇 Tsim Sha Tsui

SHAMROCK

Good-value and no-frills with an economical restaurant. Buses are on the doorstep, and you're close to the MTR.
➕ F5 ✉ 223 Nathan Road, Yau Ma Tei ☎ 2735 2271; fax 2736 354; e-mail shamrock@iohk.com 🚇 Jordan

STANFORD HILL VIEW

Small quiet hotel right in the newest night spot in town. Shuttle service to the airport train, baby-sitting, café and bar.
➕ F6 ✉ 13–17 Observatory Road, Tsim Sha Tsui ☎ 2722 7822; www.stanfordhillview.com 🚇 Tsim Sha Tsui

HOTEL TIPS

A travel agent should be able to obtain sizable discounts on the room rates in the luxury and mid-range hotels and may offer special winter rates to attract customers. Try to get a breakfast buffet included because it is often a substantial repast.

Budget Accommodations

CHUNGKING MANSIONS

For many years the Mecca for budget travelers, Chungking Mansions in Tsim Sha Tsui, may just have reached its long overdue sell-by date. Still the cheapest place to stay in Hong Kong the disadvantages of the cramped, inadequate elevators and heavily populated staircases outweigh the financial savings. Lots of the accommodations now caters to long-stay immigrant workers and the backpackers who wander in there look a little frazzled. A better place to check out is Mirador Mansions (see Garden Hostel this page), just as central but lots airier and well looked after.

HONG KONG ISLAND

ALISAN GUEST HOUSE

These 21 rooms are on fifth floor of block in Causeway Bay. All rooms have private showers and lavatories and air-conditioning. Friendly owners.

➕ G8 ✉ Flat A 5/F Hoito Court, 275 Gloucester Road, Causeway Bay ☎ 2838 0762 🚇 Causeway Bay

NOBLE HOSTEL

A reliable establishment offering rooms with both shared and private bath. A double with private bathroom at HK$340–$HK360 is a gem of a bargain.

➕ G8 ✉ Flat A3, 17/F, 27 Paterson Street, Causeway Bay ☎ 2576 6148; fax 2577 0847 🚇 Causeway Bay

WANG FAT HOSTEL

The best value for budget accommodations on the island. A series of rooms in a block of flats, most with private bath, phone, fridge and TV. Communal kitchen and laundry.

➕ G8 ✉ Flat A2 3/F Paterson Building, 47 Paterson Street, Causeway Bay ☎ 2895 1015; www.wangfathostel.com 🚇 Causeway Bay

KOWLOON

BOOTH LODGE

Named after the founder of the Salvation Army (which operates the place). This hotel is well run, with clean rooms, efficient service and a small café.

➕ F5 ✉ 11 Wing Sing Lane, Yau Ma Tei ☎ 2771 9266; fax 2385 1140 🚇 Yau Ma Tei

CARITAS BLANCHI LODGE

Tidy, clean, well run and friendly. Facilities are limited, just a laundry and restaurants.

➕ F5 ✉ 4 Cliff Road, Yau Ma Tei ☎ 2388 1111; fax 2770 6669 🚇 Yau Ma Tei

CARITAS LODGE (BOUNDARY STREET)

Basic and roomy with a coffee shop, laundry facilities and some triple rooms.

➕ G3 ✉ 134 Boundary Street, Kowloon ☎ 2339 3777; fax 2338 2864 🚇 Prince Edward, then bus 2D

GARDEN HOSTEL

Mirador Mansions is fast becoming an upscale replacement for Chungking Mansions. Great place for meeting other backpackers and swapping stories. You have a choice of shower or bath and an open terrace. If it is full there are other hostels in the same building.

➕ F6 ✉ Flat 4, 3/F Mirador Mansion, 58–62 Nathan Road, Tsim Sha Tsui ☎ 2311 1183; fax 2721 2085 🚇 Tsim Sha Tsui

STAR GUEST HOUSE

Along with its sister hostel, at No.36 Cameron Road, this well-run guest house is very reasonably priced. Some rooms have showers. Reserve in advance

➕ G3 ✉ Flat B 6/F 21 Cameron Road, Tsim Sha Tsui ☎ 2339 3777; fax 2338 2864 🚇 Tsim Sha Tsui

HONG KONG
travel facts

Essential Facts *90–91*

Getting Around *91–92*

Media & Communications *92*

Emergencies *92–93*

Language *93*

ESSENTIAL FACTS

Customs regulations
- Duty-free allowance is 1 liter of spirits and 200 cigarettes.
- Export and import licences are required for any amount of ivory taken out of the country.

Departure tax
- Anyone over 12 years old pays HK$120 (in Hong Kong dollars only). This is usually included in the price of your airline ticket.

Electricity
- The current is 200/220 volts, 50 cycles alternating current (AC).
- Most wall outlets take three square prongs; some older ones take three large round prongs.
- US appliances require a converter and a plug adaptor.

Etiquette
- Hong Kong is a fast city so don't be surprised when people push, shove and jump the line or fail to line up at all.
- Shaking hands is common practice, as is the exchanging of business cards, presented with both hands.
- A service charge is usually added to restaurant bills, but the staff do not get this money as tips so an extra 10 percent is expected. Round up taxi fares to the next dollar or two.

Lavatories
- Most are Western style.
- Hotels are the best places to find clean lavatories.
- In older places, on public transportation, lavatories are often the squat type.
- Public lavatories are free.
- Always carry a packet of tissues.

Lone travelers
- Hong Kong is similar to, and often safer than, European or North American cities; take commonsense precautions.
- Public transportation at night is as safe as during the day.

Money matters
- Traveler's checks can often be used as payment or cashed at banks or moneychangers. Always check the exchange rate before making any transaction; banks offer the best rates.
- Credit cards—Visa, Access (MasterCard), American Express and Diners Club—are widely accepted for purchases in shops and restaurants. In small shops check commission is not added—this is illegal.
- Credit cards can be used to obtain cash from banks and ATM machines. Some Hong Kong Bank teller machines provide 24-hour HK$ withdrawal facilities for Visa and MasterCard holders. Amex holders have the same facility at some Jetco ATMs, as well as the Express ATMs.

National holidays
Dates of the Chinese lunar festivals vary from year to year.
- 1 January: New Year's Day.
- Late January or early February: Chinese New Year.
- Good Friday and Easter Monday.
- Early April: Ching Ming Festival.
- Early April/early May: Buddha's birthday.
- 1 May: Labor Day.
- Mid- to late-June: Dragon Boat Festival.
- 1 July: Hong Kong SAR Establishment Day.

- Early or mid-August: Sino-Japanese War Victory Day.
- Late September or early October: Mid-Autumn Festival.
- 1 and 2 October: China National Day.
- Mid- to late October: Cheung Yeung Festival.
- 25 and 26 December: Christmas Day and Boxing Day.

Opening hours

- Offices: Mon–Fri 9–5, Sat 9–1
- Banks: Mon–Fri 9–4.30, Sat 9–12.30
- Post offices: Mon–Fri 8–6, Sat 8–2
- Shops: Daily 10–6, often 10–9 in tourist areas.

Places of worship

- Protestant Evangelical Community Church ✉ 4th floor YMCA, Salisbury Road, Tsim Sha Tsui ☎ 2369 2211
- The Roman Catholic Cathedral ✉ 16 Cairn Road, Mid Levels, Hong Kong Island ☎ 2810 4066
- Jewish Ohel Leah Synagogue ✉ 70 Robinson Road, Central ☎ 2857 6095
- Kowloon Mosque ✉ Kowloon Park ☎ 2724 0095

Student travelers

- There are few discounts for ISIC (International Student Identity Card) holders.
- The Student Travel Bureau ✉ Room 1021, 10/F, Star House, Tsim Sha Tsui ☎ 2730 3269 dispenses a free booklet detailing retail outlets with student discounts.
- Some places of interest have a reduced student admission.

Tourist information

- The Hong Kong Tourist Board (HKTB) has two offices: ✉ Star Ferry Concourse, Tsim Sha Tsui

🕐 Mon–Fri 8–6, Sat, Sun, public holidays 9–5 ✉ G/F The Center, Queen's Road, Central 🕐 Daily 8–6
- For telephone information: ☎ 2508 1234, daily 8–6
- The tourist board has developed the Quality Tourism Services scheme as a pledge of service excellence. Look for establishments displaying the QTS logo.

GETTING AROUND

Buses

- Traveling on buses is not really recommended, but in the event of using one, note the fixed fare is marked on the bus as you enter and pay; no change is given.

Taxis

- The flagfare is HK$15 and after a mile (2km) the fare increases by HK$1.40 for every 210 yds (200m). There is a HK$5 additional charge if a taxi is booked by phone and comes to your pick-up point.
- A "For Hire" sign is displayed in the windscreen; at night a "Taxi" sign is lit up on the roof.
- Taxis are not supposed to stop at bus stops or on a yellow line.

Trains

- ► 7.

Trams

- Trams run only on Hong Kong Island's north side—but the route between Kennedy Town in the west and Causeway Bay in the east is useful.
- Destinations are marked on the front in English.
- The fixed fare of HK$2 is dropped in the paybox when leaving the tram.

91

Travel discounts

- For the MTR, KCR, buses, some ferries and several other forms of public transportation, you can buy an Octopus ticket. It costs HK$150, for which you get a little over HK$100 worth of travel. The other HK$50 is refundable when you leave. You can recharge the card as often as you want at any ticket office. It will save you finding change for bus journeys and lining up for tickets in the busy MTR. Check your ticket balance at any railway station or look at the machine as you go through the barrier. Further discounts are available for students, senior citizens and children.

- For more information about getting around ➤ 7.

MEDIA & COMMUNICATIONS

Newspapers and Magazines

- International newspapers and magazines are available in bookshops, hotel kiosks and newsagents on street corners. The newsagent outside the Star Ferry terminal in Tsim Sha Tsui and the bookshop next to the ferry terminal in Central have a good selection.
- There are two English-language daily newspapers: the broadsheet *South China Morning Post* and the tabloid *Hong Kong Standard*.
- For entertainment listings look for the free, bi-weekly *HK Magazine* or *BC Magazine*.

Post offices

- The General Post Office on Hong Kong Island is next to the Star Ferry Concourse in Central.

- In Kowloon, the main post office is at 10 Middle Road, off the lower end of Nathan Road.
- Letters and postcards to destinations outside Southeast Asia cost HK$3.10 for the first 10g, plus HK$1.20 for each additional gram.
- The Speedpost service (☎ 2921 2277) cuts the usual five-day service to Europe or North America by about half.

Telephones

- Local calls are free from private homes. Public phones charge HK$1 per call and sometimes only take HK$2 coins without giving change. Pressing the "FC" (follow-on call) button before hanging up allows a second call.
- Phonecards, available in denominations of HK$70 and HK$100 at 7–Eleven stores and lots of shops, are easier to use, especially for International Direct Dialling calls.
- Some telephone boxes accept only phonecards or only coins.
- For IDD calls, dial 001, followed by the country code and then the area code (minus any initial 0) and number. Dial 013 for information about international calls.
- To call Hong Kong from abroad dial 00 852, then the 8-digit number.

EMERGENCIES

Emergency phone numbers

- Police/Fire/Ambulance ☎ 999

Embassies and consulates

- Australia ✉ 23rd and 24th Floors, Harbour Centre, 25 Harbour Road, Wan Chai ☎ 2827 8881

- Canada ✉ 11th–14th Floors, Tower One, Exchange Square, 8 Connaught Place, Central ☎ 2810 4321
- Germany ✉ 21st Floor, United Centre, 95 Queensway, Central ☎ 2105 8788
- UK ✉ 1 Supreme Court Road, Admiralty ☎ 2901 3000
- US ✉ 26 Garden Road, Central ☎ 2523 9011

Lost property

- ✉ Admiralty MTR station
  ⊕ Mon–Sat 8–7 ☎ 2861 0020

Medical treatment

- Outpatient departments of public or private hospitals provide emergency treatment.
- Private doctors (see Yellow Pages) charge HK$150 per visit on average. This usually includes three days' medication.
- Public hospitals:
  Queen Mary Hospital ✉ Pok Fu Lam Road, Hong Kong Island ☎ 2855 3111
  Queen Elizabeth Hospital ✉ Wylie Road, Yau Ma Tei, Kowloon ☎ 2958 8888
  Kwong Wah Hospital ✉ 25 Waterloo Road, Yau Ma Tei, Kowloon ☎ 2332 2311
- Private hospitals: Hong Kong Central ✉ 1B Lower Albert Road, Central, Hong Kong Island ☎ 2522 3141
  Adventist ✉ 40 Stubbs Road, Wan Chai, Hong Kong Island ☎ 2574 6211
  Baptist ✉ 222 Waterloo Road, Kowloon Tong ☎ 2337 4141

Medicines

- Watson's and Manning's are the biggest chain stores dispensing medicines (see "Chemists" in the Yellow Pages) and are usually open until 8pm.
- A full range of pharmaceuticals is readily available, but you should bring special medicines with you.

Sensible precautions

- Hong Kong is very crowded, night and day, and professional thieves capitalize on this.
- Keep wallets and purses secure.
- Keep traveler's checks separate from the invoice that lists their numbers.
- Don't leave valuables where you can't see them at all times.
- Keep travel documents and money in a hotel safe.

LANGUAGE

- Hong Kong has two official languages: Cantonese and English. While English is spoken widely in business circles and tourist areas, is not always understood. It's best to get the hotel receptionist to write down your destination in Chinese.
- A few words of Cantonese go a long way in establishing rapport—and off the beaten track they may prove useful.

Can you speak English? neih wuih mwuih gong ying mahn?
good morning jóu sahn
how are you? néih hou ma?
hello (only on the phone) wai! (pronounced "why")
thank you (for a favor) mgòi
thank you (for a gift) dò jeh
please mgòi
excuse me mgòi
I'm sorry deui mjyuh
yes haih or hou
no mhaih or mhou
where? bin douh?
how many/how much? géi dō?
how much is it? géi dō chin?
airport fèi gèi chèung
bus bā si
tram dihn chè
what time is it? géi dim jung?

93

Index

A

accommodations 86–88
afternoon tea 69
airport 6
antique shops 73
Apliu Street 56
architecture 52–53
Art, Museum of 45
arts and crafts 72
arts venues 80–81
Astronomy, Museum of 44

B

Bank of China Building 38
Bank of China Tower 38, 40, 52
banks 90
bargaining 19
bargain bazaars 79
beaches 54
bird markets 56
Bonham Strand 32
Botanical Gardens 35
Bowen Road 22
buses 7, 91

C

cameras 76
Canton 21
Cantonese food 64
cash machines 90
Central Market 34
Central Plaza 52
Chater Garden 38
Chater House 58
Che Kai Shan (Victoria Peak) 30
Chek Lap Kok Airport 6
Cheung Chau 54, 62
children's entertainment 60
China Folk Culture Village 21
Chinese New Year 4
Chinese opera 81
Chinese University of Hong Kong Art Gallery 61
chopsticks 65
Chungking Mansions 88
City Hall complex 61
City Plaza 58, 60
climate 4
clothing stores 77–79
computer stores 75
concerts and shows 81
country parks 54
credit cards 90
crime 93
customs regulations 90
cybercafés 5

D

departure tax 90
dim sum 64
disabilities, visitors with 7
dragon-boat races 4
Dragon Shopping Centre 58

E

electricity 90
electronic goods 76
embassies and consulates 92–93
emergencies 92–93
emporia 72
entertainment 80–85
entry requirements 6
etiquette 90
events and festivals 4
Excelsior Hotel 53, 86
Exchange Square 36
excursions 20–21
    Lantau Island 20, 26
    Macau 20
    New Territories 21
    People's Republic of China 21

F

Fa Yuen Street 56
factory outlets 79
fashion shops 77–78
feng shui 52, 53
ferries 40, 62
Flagstaff House 61
flower markets 56, 57
food and drink
    chopsticks 65
    dim sum 64
    eating out 64–71
    floating restaurants 64, 65
    pubs 85
fortune-tellers 31, 33
free attractions 61

G

geomancers 52
ginseng 32
golf 82
Government House 35
green spaces 54
Guangzhou 21
gweilos 13

H

handover, the 17
Harbour City 59
harbour cruises 20
helicopter tours 62
heritage tour 20
History, Museum of 41
Hollywood Road 73

Hong Kong & Shanghai Banking Corporation Building 38, 53
Hong Kong Convention & Exhibition Centre 53
Hong Kong Cultural Centre 53
Hong Kong Racing Musem 61
Hong Kong Park 39
Hong Kong Railway Museum 21
Hong Kong Science Museum 60
Hong Kong Trail 54
hostels 88
hospitals 93
hostess clubs 24
hotels 86–88
Hung Sheng Temple 55

I

Ice Palace 60
IFC Mall 58
International Finance Centre 53
international newspapers 92

J

jade market 43
Japanese food 67
Jardine's Bazaar 57
jewelry and watches 74
jogging 82
journeys 62

K

Kowloon–Canton Railway 7
Kowloon Park 61
Kowloon Walled City Park 49

L

Ladies' Market 57
Lamma Island 54
Landmark Shopping Centre 58, 77, 78
Lan Kwai Fong 84
language 93
Lantau Island 20, 26
lavatories 90
Law Uk Folk Museum 61
Legislative Council Building 38
Lei Cheng Uk Museum 37
Li Yuen Street 57
Litt Shing Kung 33
lone travelers 90

lost property 93
Lover's Stone Garden 22
Lu Pan Temple 55

M

Macau 20, 55
magazines 92
Mai Po Marshes 27
Man Mo Temple, Central 33
Man Mo Temple, Tai Po 20, 21
Ma On Shan Country Park 54
maps 7
Marble Road Market 57
markets 22, 34, 43, 56–57
media 92
medical treatment 93
medicines 93
Mid Levels 22, 62
Military Cemetery, Stanley 50
Mo Tat Wan beach 54
money 6, 90
MTR (Mass Transit Railway) 7, 92
Museum of Art 45
Museum of Astronomy 44
Museum of History 41
Museum of Teaware 39
music, live 84

N

national holidays 90–91
neighborhoods 10
New Territories 21
New World Centre 58
newspapers 92
night market 43
nightclubs 83
nightlife 24, 83–85
nightlife (Hong Kong Island) 24, 84
nightlife (Kowloon) 24, 85

O

Ocean Park 42
Ocean Terminal 58
Odditorium 30
Omnimax Theatre 44
One & Two International Finace Centre 53
opening hours 91
opera, Chinese 81

P

Pacific Place 58, 77, 78
passports and visas 6
Patten, Chris 17
Peak Galleria 30

Peak Tram 30
People's Republic of China 21
places of worship 91
Po Lin Buddha 26
Po Lin Monastery 26
Pok Fu Lam Country Park 54
Pok Fu Lam Public Riding School 60
Police Museum 61
population 11
Possession Street 23
postal services and post offices 91, 92
public transportation 7, 91–92
pubs 85

R

Railway Museum. Tai Po 61
religions 55
Repulse Bay 58
restaurants 64–71
Roman Catholic cathedral 55, 91

S

Sai Kung Peninsula 54
St. John's Cathedral 55, 91
St. Stephen's Beach 50
safety 93
Sam Tung Uk Museum 28
SARS 12
seasons 4
Sha Tin 47, 76
Shek O 62
Shenzen 21
Sheung Shui 21
Sheung Wan Market 23
Sheung Yiu Folk Park Museum, Saiking 61
shopping 18–19, 72–79, 91
shopping malls 58–59
Shun Tak Centre 59
sightseeing tours 20, 62
skating rinks 60
Soho 84
Space Museum 44
Splendid China theme park 21
sport 82
Stanley 50
Star Ferry 40
statistical information 11
Statue Square 38
student travelers 91
swimming 82
Symphony of Lights 46

T

Tai Ping Shan Street 31
Tai Tam Country Park 54
taxis 91
Teaware, Museum of 39
telephone numbers, emergency 92–3
telephones 92
temperatures 4
Temple Street 43
temples 55
Ten Thousand Buddhas Temple 47
theaters 80
ticket outlets 80
tickets (travel) 92
time differences 4
Times Square 59, 78
Tin Hau Temples
  Causeway Bay 55
  Kowloon 55
  Repulse Bay 55
  Stanley 50
tipping 90
tourist information 91
trains 7, 92
trams 62, 91
travel discounts 92
travel insurance 7
traveler's checks 90
traveling to Hong Kong 6
triads 14
typhoons 4

U

University Museum 29
Upper Lascar Row 57

V

Victoria Park 56
Victoria Peak (Che Kai Shan) 30

W

walks 22–23
Wan Chai 22
watches 74
websites 5
Western Market 23, 57
Wing Lok Street 23
Wong Tai Sin Temple 48
work ethic 15
World War II 16

Y

Ying Sin Kwun Temple 21

Z

Zoological Gardens 35

CityPack
Hong Kong *Top 25*

ABOUT THE AUTHOR

Joseph Levy Sheenan lived in Hong Kong for a number of years and now lives in London. He has travelled extensively in southeast Asia and has contributed to several guide books on the region. He always enjoys returning to Hong Kong and he would like to thank Elliot Bloomfied for his assistance on the research trip for this edition.

Author *Joseph Levy Sheenan*   **Revision Management** *Apostrophe S Limited*
Cover Design *Fabrizio La Rocca, Tigist Getachew*

A CIP catalogue record for this book is available from the British Library.

ISBN-10: 0 7495 4355 8
ISBN-13: 978 0 7495 4355 6

All rights reserved. No part of this publication may be reproduced, stored in a retrieval system or transmitted in any form or by any means—electronic, photocopying, recording or otherwise—unless the written permission of the publishers has been obtained beforehand. This book may not be lent, resold, hired out or otherwise disposed of by way of trade in any form of binding or cover other than that in which it is published, without the prior consent of the publishers.

The contents of this publication are believed correct at the time of printing. Nevertheless, the publishers cannot be held responsible for any errors or omissions or for changes in the details given in this guide or for the consequences of any reliance on the information provided by the same. This does not affect your statutory rights. Assessments of attractions, hotels, restaurants and so forth are based upon the author's own personal experience and, therefore, descriptions given in this guide necessarily contain an element of subjective opinion which may not reflect the publishers' opinion or dictate a reader's own experiences on another occasion. We have tried to ensure accuracy in this guide, but things do change and we would be grateful if readers would advise us of any inaccuracies they may encounter.

Published by AA Publishing, a trading name of Automobile Association Developments Limited, whose registered office is Southwood East, Apollo Rise, Farnborough, Hampshire, GU14, 0JW. Registered number 1878835.

© **AUTOMOBILE ASSOCIATION DEVELOPMENTS LIMITED 1996, 1999, 2002, 2005**
First published 1996. Revised second edition 1999. Revised third edition 2002.
Revised fourth edition 2005.

Colour separation by Keenes, Andover
Manufactured by Hang Tai D&P Limited, Hong Kong

ACKNOWLEDGEMENTS

The Automobile Association would like to thank the following photographers, libraries and associations for their assistance in the preparation of this title.

Roger Fletcher/Alamy 49; Art Directors and TRIP Photo Library 60; Hong Kong Tourist Board 1t, 2, 4, 6, 8cl, 8bl, 8c, 8b, 8/9, 9c, 9cr, 9b, 10/11, 11t, 12c, 13t, 13cl, 13cr, 14c, 15, 17, 18c, 18/19, 19, 23, 24cl, 24c, 24cr, 27, 53; Museum of History, Hong Kong 41t, 41b; Photodisc Front Cover (food); Symphony of Light 46t, 46b; Stockbyte 5; Museum & Art Gallery, University of Kong Kong 29; World Pictures 26t, 26b

The remaining pictures are held in the Association's own library (AA WORLD TRAVEL LIBRARY) and were taken by Alex Kourprianoff, with the exception of Front Cover (tram, boat) Back Cover ct, cb, 1b, 7tl, 7tc, 16/17, 21, 22b which were taken by Nigel Hicks.

A01992	
Fold-out map	© RV Reise- und Verkehrsverlag Munich · Stuttgart
	© Cartography: GeoData
Transport map	© TCS, Aldershot, England

TITLES IN THE CITYPACK SERIES
• Amsterdam • Bangkok • Barcelona • Beijing • Berlin • Boston • Brussels & Bruges • Chicago • Dublin •
• Florence • Hong Kong • Lisbon • London • Los Angeles • Madrid • Melbourne • Miami • Milan •
• Montréal • Munich • Naples • New York • Paris • Prague • Rome • San Francisco • Seattle • Shanghai •
• Singapore • Sydney • Tokyo • Toronto • Venice • Vienna • Washington DC •

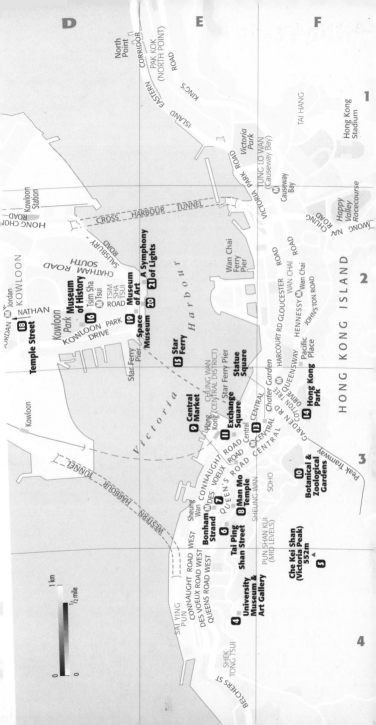

D   **E**   **F**

North Point

PAK KOK (NORTH POINT) ROAD

ISLAND EASTERN CORRIDOR

KING'S ROAD

TAI HANG

Hong Kong Stadium

1

Victoria Park

TUNG LO WAN (Causeway Bay)

Causeway Bay

Happy Valley Racecourse

WONG NAI CHUNG ROAD

VICTORIA PARK ROAD

CROSS HARBOUR TUNNEL

KOWLOON Station

HONG CHONG ROAD

KOWLOON

NATHAN ROAD

CHATHAM ROAD SOUTH

SALISBURY ROAD

Kowloon Park

Museum of History 19

20 Museum of Art

21 A Symphony of Lights

Wan Chai Ferry Pier

WAN CHAI ROAD

GLOUCESTER ROAD

HENNESSY Ⓜ Wan Chai ROAD

JOHNSTON ROAD

HONG KONG ISLAND

2

JORDAN Ⓜ Jordan

18 **Temple Street**

KOWLOON PARK DRIVE

Tsim Sha Tsui

TSIM SHA TSUI Ⓜ TSIM SHA TSUI ROAD

17 Space Museum 16

Star Ferry Pier

Star Ferry 15

13 Star Ferry

CHUNG WAN (CENTRAL DISTRICT)

14 Hong Kong Park

Pacific Place

HARCOURT RD

QUEENSWAY

COTTON TREE DRIVE

GARDEN RD

Kowloon

Victoria   Harbour

Hong Kong Ⓜ (Central District)

Statue Square

Star Ferry Pier Central

Chater Garden

CENTRAL Ⓜ CENTRAL

9 **Central Market**

11 Exchange Square

12

CENTRAL ROAD

3

WESTERN HARBOUR TUNNEL

Sheung Wan

CONNAUGHT ROAD

DES VOEUX ROAD

QUEEN'S ROAD

6 **Bonham Strand**

7 **Tai Ping Shan Street**

8 Man Mo Temple

SHEUNG WAN

SOHO

PUN SHAN KUI (MID-LEVELS)

10 Botanical & Zoological Gardens

Peak Tramway

SAT YING PUN

CONNAUGHT ROAD WEST

DES VOEUX ROAD WEST

QUEENS ROAD WEST

4 **University Museum & Art Gallery**

5 Che Kei Shan (Victoria Peak) 552m ▲

4

BELCHERS ST

SHEK TONG TSUI

0   1 km

0   ½ mile

AA CITYPack

Hong Kong

It's up to date and easy to use.

Expert travel writer Joe Levy Sheehan tells you all you need to know about Hong Kong.

"The separate map in AA CityPack is brilliant"
You Magazine, Mail on Sunday

- Top 25 sights in Hong Kong
- The best of the rest
- Restaurants – all prices and cuisines
- Living Hong Kong – the magazine
- The best walks
- Music, nightclubs, theatres, bars
- Shopping choices
- Street map and index

The AA's travel experts have created this guide to help you make the most of your trip. Visit www.theAA.com/bookshop for more AA travel information.

Just **AA** sk...

Top 25 Sights

Shopping

Eating Out

Nightlife

Street Map

ISBN 0-7495-4355-8

9 780749 543556

£6.99